THE DEMAND FOR PUBLIC STORAGE OF WHEAT IN PAKISTAN:

Thomas C. Pinckney

Research Report 77
International Food Policy Research Institute
December 1989

Library of Congress Cataloging-
in-Publication Data

Pinckney, Thomas C.
    The demand for public storage of wheat in
Pakistan.

    (Research report / International Food Policy
Research Institute ; 77)
    "December 1989."
    Includes bibliographical references.
    1. Wheat—Storage—Economic aspects—
Pakistan. 2. Wheat trade—Pakistan. I. Title.
II. Series: Research report (International Food
Policy Research Institute) ; 77.

HD9049.W5P365 1989   338.1'6   89-26752
ISBN 0-89629-079-4

STP

CONTENTS

TABLES

ILLUSTRATIONS

FOREWORD

The governments of many less-developed countries are involved in the storage of staple foods. The most common justification for such storage is the presumed unfavorable effect on consumers and producers of year-to-year variability in production. In this report, Thomas C. Pinckney adds to IFPRI's long history of research on interannual supply stabilization issues by extending earlier analyses of Kenya, the Sahel, and other countries to Pakistan. Techniques developed in the Kenya research report are modified and expanded to clarify which types of trade and price interventions are most effective and efficient for stabilizing consumption.

In contrast to interannual storage issues, government's role in seasonal storage, including the effect of within-year price policy on the demand for public storage, is frequently neglected. This study, together with a recent report on Bangladesh, points out the importance of this component of storage for the size of government storage facilities and expected cost to the government. For Pakistan, this research demonstrates that relatively small adjustments in seasonal price policy have a much greater impact on fiscal cost and demand for storage facilities than the specified adjustments in inter-annual policies.

Research on these issues is continuing in southern Africa, where the interaction between supply stabilization policies of different countries in the region is the focus of analysis.

John W. Mellor

Washington, D.C.
December 1989

ACKNOWLEDGMENTS

This report presents results of research conducted over three years at IFPRI with funds from USAID Project No. 391-0491-C-00-5033-00. Thanks are due to John Mellor and Alberto Valdés for entrusting a researcher fresh out of graduate school with major responsibilities in a large project.

My coauthors on earlier versions of this report—Naved Hamid, Suzanne Gnaegy, Alberto Valdés, and Marshall Klaus—were stimulating and helpful friends throughout the project. Suzanne and Marshall provided able research assistance whether my request was for mundane data collection or professional feedback on the research program.

In Pakistan, the participants at several workshops raised helpful questions and continually guided our research in directions that would be helpful for policymakers. There are too many to name, but those who were particularly helpful include Sartaj Aziz, Inam ul Haq, Zakir Hussain, A. H. Maan, Barry Primm, Tom Olsen, and Pat Peterson.

The present manuscript profited greatly from comments by Rafael Celis, Raisuddin Ahmed, and two especially helpful anonymous reviewers.

Many thanks also to colleagues at IFPRI and other institutions who discussed various aspects of the project during my tenure at the institute.

Thomas C. Pinckney

1

SUMMARY

Many governments are concerned about stabilizing supplies and prices of staple foods to avoid shortages and political difficulties. This requires intervention in the market, most often through procurement and releases of the staples. Some amount of public stockholding is required, at least in the short term, in order to intervene effectively. This study develops a methodology for estimating the total demand for government storage from three different sources and applies the methodology to wheat in Pakistan. The analysis begins with a description of Pakistan's wheat economy and prospects for future growth of supply and demand. Expected growth is on the order of 3.3 percent per year, with the country remaining self-sufficient at prices that stay below import parity. The demand for storage should increase at approximately the same rate.

The study continues with a categorization of the different reasons why stocks may be held, and then proceeds to calculate the size of the three different components of stockholding. In the process, considerable insight is gained into the nature of efficient storage, trade, and price policies; trade-offs are measured between interannual price variability and fiscal cost and between the seasonal price spread and fiscal cost; and estimates are made of the minimum amount of stock that should trigger imports month by month. The resulting figure for storage capacity is highly sensitive to the size of the within-year gap between the procurement price and the release price.

The three reasons for government stockholding are to move wheat from surplus to deficit years; to move wheat from surplus to deficit seasons; and to ensure a smooth flow of supplies at all times, especially when imports are on order but not yet available domestically. These three components of storage policy can be termed interannual supply stabilization stocks, seasonal stocks, and import buffer stocks.

Interannual supply stabilization is commonly cited as the primary purpose of government stockholding. Production varies from year to year in ways that cannot be anticipated. Since Pakistan is self-sufficient in wheat at prevailing prices in a normal production year, production variability can lead to exportable surpluses in one year, followed by imports in the next year. The government loses money in such circumstances, since there are large differences between import and export parity prices. The government has the option, then, of storing some portion of an exportable surplus and releasing these stocks in deficit years.

Despite Pakistan's relatively low level of production instability, price variability would be fairly high in the absence of government intervention in the market. A nonintervention model estimates that harvest-time procurement prices would be higher than Rs95 per 40 kilograms in one out of six years, and lower than Rs65 in one out of six years. Given this rationale for government intervention, an optimizing model is built allowing for different relative preferences between the government objectives of lowering fiscal expenditure and lowering price and consumption variability.

Stabilizing supplies by holding stocks across years turns out to cost more money than it saves on average. Regardless of the degree of government preference for price stability, the *efficient policies do not hold interannual supply stabilization stocks unless the world price for wheat falls below US$80 per metric ton.*

Given the low likelihood of such a dramatic fall in world prices, the expected benefits of building additional storage capacity do not come close to paying for construction costs. Consequently, *no capacity should be added to government storage to accommodate interannual supply stabilization stocks,* although in years of abundant supplies and low world prices some stocks of this type could efficiently be held if storage space is available.

In addition to holding no stocks, the efficient policies allow some flexibility in official prices in response to changes in the world price and domestic production. Since fiscal expenditures fall as official prices become more flexible, there is a trade-off between the government's objectives of lowering expenditures and stabilizing prices. For example, a policy that holds harvest-time prices between Rs73 and Rs87 per 40 kilograms is expected to cost about Rs200 million (US$11 million) less annually than a policy that holds those prices between Rs78.90 and Rs81.10.

The second component of demand for public storage is for seasonal stocks. The size of public seasonal storage is dependent on the relative importance of the government and the private sector in moving wheat from harvest time to the months preceding the next harvest. A model of private storage behavior is developed to test the consequences of changing the gap between the procurement and release prices.

The average level of procurement in a normal production year is shown to be sensitive to government seasonal price policy. Government policy affects private storage primarily through its effect on the seasonal pattern of wholesale prices, and thus on price expectations within the crop year.

In the past, prices have risen about 18 percent from a low in May/June/July to a peak in December/January/February, or about Rs14.00 per kilogram at current prices. Using 1987/88 prices, if the government were to buy all that was offered at the procurement price and sell all that was demanded at the release price, the seasonal price rise would be limited to little more than Rs3.20. This could lead to decreased private storage and higher levels of procurement—and larger losses—by the government.

This concern would not be an issue if private storage were small or insensitive to expected changes in price. However, estimates in this report show that *private storage at the end of July has been no less than 5 million tons* for each of the last several years. Moreover, private storage has been quite sensitive to expected changes in price. A supply-of-storage model is developed and estimated showing that the larger the expected seasonal price rise, the more private agents in Pakistan have held in the past. Thus, it is reasonable to conclude that any government policy that lowers the expected seasonal price rise will increase government procurement.

Expected costs of a narrow gap between the procurement and release prices are high. On average *the government saves about Rs100 million annually and 100,000 tons of storage capacity for every 1 paisa per kilogram increase in the gap between the procurement and release prices.*

The third component of demand for public storage, import-buffer stocks, can be further broken down into two elements. First, stocks must be sufficient to allow for some wheat to be in transit and in godowns waiting to be sold without producing any supply disruptions. One month of expected offtakes for this component is more than adequate. Second, stocks must be sufficient to provide offtakes for four succeeding months if it is discovered that imports are required. To ensure that this component of demand is met, 3.5 million tons must be stored in early August.

Combining these three components of the demand for storage yields different levels of public storage capacity, depending on the gap between the procurement and release prices. With the 1987/88 gap of 8 paisa per kilogram, required capacity is 5.4 million tons in 1988, rising to 8.2 million tons in the year 2000. With a gap of 30 paisa, required capacity falls to 3.5 million tons in 1988 and 5.3 million tons in 2000.

Five policy changes are recommended in addition to the estimation of storage capacity. In order of importance, these are choosing a gap between the procurement and release prices that takes account of the large cost savings; holding no interannual supply stabilization stocks; introducing some responsiveness of official prices to production size; introducing responsiveness of official prices to world prices; and changing the law that allows the government to seize private stocks in an emergency.

Each of these changes would improve the efficiency of the wheat marketing system in Pakistan. The degree to which seasonal and interannual prices are allowed to fluctuate, however, will be based on the relative preferences of the government for reduced fiscal expenditures and price stability.

All these policy changes except the second—holding no interannual supply stabilization stocks—are relevant to other countries that intervene in cereal markets. Countries with higher levels of production variability are more likely to gain from holding interannual supply stabilization stocks than Pakistan. The other aspects of policy design, however, should hold qualitatively across countries.

2

INTRODUCTION

The Rationale for Storage

The price and availability of a country's primary staple food are of critical concern to its government. Rapid increases in price or periods of unavailability can lead to calorie deprivation, real-income declines, and political crises. Thus, most governments take measures to moderate price fluctuations and to ensure supplies through some intervention in the market.

If the government is to have an impact on prices or availability during a shortage, it is necessary to increase supplies reaching the market. This requires moving the commodity from surplus to deficit regions, or from surplus to deficit time periods. The surplus "region" may be the world market, with imports enhancing domestic supply. Often governments or parastatal organizations store, transport, and import or export the staple food for these purposes; alternatively, they may conduct policies that encourage the private sector to perform the activities.

Such activities are typically expensive for governments. Storage of foodgrains, in particular, requires both a high capital cost up front to build proper facilities and high costs each year to hold the stock (typically 15-25 percent annually of the value of the stock). Thus, there is a trade-off: more storage space and higher stock levels allow for more timely and effective government intervention, but both result in rapidly escalating costs. Basic economic principles imply that the degree of government involvement should stop at the point where the added security is not worth the added cost. The statement is simple; defining and measuring the added security and the added costs are quite complex.

Moreover, the problem with attempting to "buy" too much security is not limited to escalating fiscal costs. If the government is attempting to defend a price policy that it is fiscally unable to enforce, the result may be higher cost and higher actual price variability than would result from allowing some official price variability. There is some evidence that this was the case in Kenya in the early 1980s (Pinckney 1988b).

Estimating the economically efficient size of government storage facilities is one important component of limiting government cost. The calculation of such a number requires an analysis of the rationale for holding stocks. There are three reasons for some market agent—possibly the government—to hold stocks of grain:[1] to move supplies from a surplus *year* to a deficit *year;* to move supplies from a surplus *season* to a deficit *season;* and to avoid any disruption in supply, particularly while imports are on order but before they arrive in the country.

In short, these three rationales can be termed the interannual, seasonal, and import-buffer storage requirements. These three distinct demands on government storage can easily be confused, yet analyzing the requirements for each must remain distinct. General considerations for analyzing them will be considered in turn.

---

[1] For another, similar analysis of the reasons for government storage, see Siamwalla 1988.

Interannual Supply Stabilization Stocks

The analysis of storage requirements for moving supplies from a surplus year to a deficit year is best begun by examining a simple identity.[2] For a particular year in any country, total supply must equal total demand. There are three possible sources of supply—production, opening stocks, and imports—and three possible sources of demand—consumption, closing stocks, and exports.[3] In equation form, this can be stated as

$$Q_t + S_{t-1} + M_t = C_t + S_t + X_t, \qquad (1)$$

where

$$
\begin{aligned}
t &= \text{year,} \\
Q &= \text{production,} \\
S &= \text{closing stocks,} \\
M &= \text{imports,} \\
C &= \text{consumption, and} \\
X &= \text{exports.}
\end{aligned}
$$

Solving for Q yields

$$Q_t = (S_t - S_{t-1}) + (X_t - M_t) + C_t. \qquad (2)$$

That is, production equals the change in stocks plus net exports plus consumption.

Equation (2) implies that when production, Q_t, fluctuates from one year to the next, at least one of the three terms on the right-hand side will also have to fluctuate. In other words, production variability *must* be translated into stock variability, trade variability, or consumption variability.

A country that is an exporter in a normal production year can buffer production fluctuations by reducing exports, provided the production shortfall is less than its usual exportable surplus. Similarly, a country that imports in a normal year can increase imports in a bad year. The production shortfall could translate into tightness in the supply of foreign exchange—and if domestic prices are not at parity with world prices, or if the exchange rate is misaligned, the country may want to adjust domestic prices in order to decrease consumption during the shortfall. In neither the case of the importer nor that of the exporter, however, is it likely that stock changes will play any role in buffering such production fluctuations. The exporter would have to forgo exports in year $t-1$ if it is to hold stocks for a possible shortfall in supply in year t. Thus, although holding stocks may allow the country to maintain exports in the face of the production shortfall in year t, the net effect is to move exports from year $t-1$ to year t, while incurring a year's worth of storage charges. Such an operation would lose money unless there were a very large movement in world prices between the years. A similar analysis would hold true for the importing country.[4]

---

[2] See Josling 1981 for a fuller discussion of this and other identities relating to food security.

[3] In this formulation, food aid is included with imports, public and private stocks are aggregated, and production is taken to be net of losses and seed.

[4] This paragraph assumes that the country is always an exporter, even in a bad year. A country such as Zimbabwe, which is an exporter of maize in a normal year but occasionally has a disastrous year and is forced to import, is more similar in this regard to a normally self-sufficient country.

The situation is considerably more complicated when a country is self-sufficient in a normal production year. This results primarily from the costs of engaging in foreign trade.[5] If a country could buy wheat in a deficit year at the U.S. Gulf Port price and sell in a surplus year at the same price, the situation would be the same as for the normal-year exporter. But for most cases, the export price is less than the U.S. Gulf Port price and the import price is more than that price. In many countries, the gap is quite large. For example, in Pakistan the difference between the import and export parity prices is about US$65 per metric ton.[6] Thus, if Pakistan has a surplus in one year and *knows* that it will be in deficit the next year, it is profitable to store the commodity for one year, since storage costs are about US$25 per ton.

The problem is that next year's crop is not known, and if the stock has to be stored for more than a couple of years, the government is losing more money than if it were to depend on imports. Thus, there is no obvious answer to the question of whether or not stocks for interannual supply stabilization should be held by a normally self-sufficient country.

The simple identity in equation (2), however, does provide at least three clues as to the general type of policy that will be most effective. First, a *"food security reserve" that ends every market year at the same level is totally ineffective* for stabilizing consumption when production is variable. In equation (2), it is the *change* in stocks that counteracts the shortfall in production. Thus, if stocks do not change, whether they begin and end the year at 0 or 3 million tons, *all* of the production decline will be translated into increased imports or decreased consumption. Such a reserve may act as an import buffer—the third type of storage requirement—but it does not stabilize consumption across years.

Second, *domestic price policy is intimately related to storage questions.* In equation (2), if domestic prices are allowed to change in response to fluctuations in production, consumption will change, leading to less need for stock or trade variability. The extent to which domestic consumption varies with domestic production is thus important in the formulation of a storage strategy.

Finally, *trade variability and stock variability can be substitutes for each other.* Thus, a country can stabilize consumption by depending totally on trade or mostly on stock changes to make up for production surpluses and shortfalls. For a wheat-consuming country, the choice between relying on one or the other should be based purely on cost after accounting for any misalignment of the exchange rate (recall that stocks to cover the delay between ordering and receiving imports are analyzed separately), as consumers have no clear preference for domestic wheat or imported wheat and the international market for wheat functions well. It is likely that the relative costs of relying on trade or stocks will vary with the world price. For white-maize-consuming countries, the situation is complicated by a preference for the domestic commodity compared with the internationally traded commodity.

Given these clues, then, the question is how much domestic prices should adjust to a production deviation, thereby allowing consumption to vary with production. Of the remaining production variability, how much should be assigned to stock variability and how much to trade variability?

---

[5] For countries where the staple food is rice or white maize, the thinness of the international market is another consideration.

[6] All tons in this report are metric tons.

The answers to these questions depend on the characteristics of the country in question. One particularly important parameter is the degree of willingness of the government to spend fiscal resources to stabilize consumption. These issues are discussed in detail in Chapter 3.

Seasonal Storage

Even if a government holds no interannual stocks, there may be a need to hold seasonal stocks if the seasonal price variability in the absence of intervention is undesirably high. There is reason to believe, however, that once a government begins to involve itself in seasonal storage, the demand for storage capacity could increase dramatically. A government that holds 10 percent of its normal production across years will cover the vast majority of shortfalls in annual production; if all production takes place in one quarter, however, a government would have to hold 75 percent of annual consumption to cover the "shortfall in supply" during the last three quarters of the year. Thus, it is likely that the primary demand for public storage will result from seasonal considerations.

Equation (2) can be generalized to make it appropriate not only to years but also to seasons. Distinguishing between private and public stocks is necessary in this context, since many private agents, including producers, hold seasonal stocks. If time period t is considered to be, say, quarters of the marketing year, after isolating consumption on the right-hand side the equation becomes

$$Q_t + (SG_{t-1} - SG_t) + (SP_{t-1} - SP_t) + (M_t - X_t) = C_t, \qquad (3)$$

where
SG = government stocks,
SP = private stocks, and
$Q_t < Q_1$ if t = 2, 3, or 4, defining quarter 1
as the primary harvesting quarter.

The equation shows that consumption equals this quarter's production plus the net decline in government stocks plus the net decline in private stocks plus net imports. The same identity holds for the annual case, the main difference being the extreme production instability, which is known ahead of time in the quarterly case. If all of the harvest takes place in the first quarter, for three quarters all consumption comes from stock drawdowns or imports.

The equation provides three important insights into the nature of seasonal stocks. First, as in the annual case, stock variability and trade variability are substitutes. The rationale for holding stocks is much stronger in the seasonal case, however, since it is known that no production will take place for three quarters and since the lag between ordering and receiving imports will be at least one full quarter. Nevertheless, a country that is a normal-year importer can reduce domestic storage costs considerably by timing imports to coincide with the preharvest period.

Price policy has a greater effect on seasonal storage than on interannual storage because of the increased importance of private stocks. Private stocks should respond to changes in expected prices. A government policy that involves increases in government stocks and decreases in the seasonal price rise may actually *lower* total stocks if the price effect on private stocks is greater than the additional government stocks. In addition, allowing seasonal prices to increase has the same effect as in the interannual case of decreasing consumption during the scarce months.

The second point to be made from the equation is the trade-off between private and public stocks: if private agents do not store wheat, all seasonal storage will have to be conducted by the government. Thus, seasonal storage issues have the potential to be extremely costly for the government in terms of operating costs and storage-space requirements.

The final point is an obvious one: seasonal storage demand is seasonal. The peak for this type of storage is immediately after the harvest, while the minimum is virtually zero immediately prior to the harvest. To the extent that the other two reasons for holding stocks have seasonal components, total storage capacity required by the government is likely to be less than the sum of the maximum requirements for each of the three types of stockholding. Thus, it will be necessary to consider the storage requirements on a monthly or quarterly basis in order to estimate accurately the total demand for government storage.

Storage for Avoiding Disruptions in Supply

This type of storage is composed of amounts that are required at any one time to be in transit or in regional stores, and the amount necessary to allow for the delay in the arrival of imports when they are necessary. Since the latter requirement is likely to be the largest in most months, the term "import-buffer stocks" is appropriate and will be used here. In some analyses, this component of storage is termed "working stocks," but that term can be confusing, since it is also used for seasonal storage in many papers.

The key questions are these: How long does it take the government to make a decision to import, including the allocation of foreign exchange? Once ordered, how long is the delay before imports arrive, are unloaded, and are available? What is the distribution of net offtake from government stocks for different months?

The last question indicates that this component of storage, like the seasonal stock component, will vary by month. Unlike the other components of storage, however, little can be said about this component before examining empirical data. This empirical analysis is presented in Chapter 5.

Storage Demand for Wheat in Pakistan

Wheat is the staple food for the vast majority of Pakistan's population, contributing almost 50 percent of total calories. The government has been involved in the wheat market for many years through procurement and release policies. Prior to planting time, the government announces a procurement price that will be effective at harvest time. Farmers are free to sell to the government at the procurement price or to private agents at any other price.

From World War II until 1987, the primary mechanism for the government to release wheat was through the ration shop system. The system was subject to much abuse and was replaced in March of 1987, with the government promising to release all of the wheat demanded at a set price (see Alderman 1988b). These policies clearly imply an important role for government storage, both within and between years.

In addition, the government controls all official foreign trade in wheat and wheat products. Although some unofficial trade in wheat takes place, these amounts are necessarily small. Thus, the government has chosen to play a major role in marketing, trading, and storing wheat.

Escalating costs and the recent change in policy toward releases have contributed to the need to understand the rationale for storage and to explore various ways of bringing the costs of wheat policy in line with the benefits of government involvement. Thus, Pakistan is a useful case study in which to analyze the demand for public storage.[7]

Chapter 3 briefly summarizes Pakistan's wheat economy and includes an examination of the primary agroclimatic zones for wheat production, a forward look at the future of Pakistan's consumption and production of wheat, and a backward look at the historical instability of wheat production. Chapters 4, 5, and 6 examine the demand for interannual supply stabilization stocks, seasonal stocks, and import buffer stocks, respectively. The final chapter draws conclusions for Pakistan and other countries concerning the demand for public storage.

---

[7] Public storage of other cereals produced and consumed in Pakistan—maize, millet, sorghum, barley, and rice—is not considered in this study. The government does not purchase the first four, and thus does not engage in public storage of them. Rice is an export crop, and thus requires a very different type of analysis. Furthermore, since rice consumption is less than one-fifth of wheat consumption, and since rice calories are considerably more expensive than wheat calories, it is unlikely that rice plays an important role in buffering supply instability of wheat, particularly for poor consumers.

3

THE SETTING OF PAKISTAN'S WHEAT ECONOMY

In order to assess the demand for public storage of wheat, it is necessary to understand the basic structure of wheat production in Pakistan. This chapter opens with a summary of the agroclimatic zones where wheat is grown, followed by brief sections on government intervention in the wheat market and supply responsiveness of wheat production. Trends in production for the country as a whole and by zone are summarized, and expected growth in consumption is examined. This is followed by an estimate of future growth in wheat production and consumption given price adjustments implied by trends in production and consumption of other major agricultural commodities. The final section considers the historical production instability.

The Structure of Wheat Production in Pakistan

Agriculture accounts for about one-fourth of Pakistan's gross domestic product (GDP), with wheat production accounting for just over one-fourth of agriculture's value added. Livestock products contribute 30 percent of agriculture's value added, with most of the rest produced by cotton, rice, and sugarcane. More than one-third of cropped acreage is planted to wheat.

The major agricultural areas of Pakistan lie in the Indus basin. Of the 31 million hectares considered suitable for cultivation, more than 20 million are cultivated; about 14 million of these cultivated hectares are in the Indus Plains. This area supplies more than 80 percent of agricultural production.

Most parts of the Indus Plains do not receive enough rainfall to support agriculture. They are exceptionally flat, however, providing some of the best land for gravity-fed irrigation in the world. During the last 130 years, more than 40,000 miles of canals have been built.[8] More recently, more than 200,000 private and public tubewells have begun to supplement canal irrigation. About 85 percent of wheat production takes place under irrigation, leaving only 15 percent for the rainfed *(barani)* areas.

There are two main cropping seasons in most of Pakistan: *kharif* (April to November) and *rabi* (November-April). Cotton, rice, maize, millets, sorghum, and sugarcane[9] are the major *kharif* crops, while wheat, oilseeds, gram, and barley are the major *rabi* crops. Of the total cropped area, 55 percent is planted in the *rabi* season and the rest in the *kharif* season. There are large interregional differences, however; in the Sind, only 42 percent of cropped land is planted in the *rabi* season.

The cropping patterns and rotations vary in different parts of the Indus Plains. Therefore, it is useful for purposes of this study to divide the country into agroclimatic

---

[8] For a fascinating account of the development of the irrigation system and the effect of partition on the system, see Michel 1967.

[9] Since sugarcane is sown in spring and harvested in winter, it is considered a *kharif* crop, but generally a second ratoon crop is also taken and therefore, in practice, it occupies the land for both seasons.

zones.[10] Since wheat is the predominant crop in the *rabi* season in virtually all areas, the primary *kharif* season crop becomes the basis for differentiating the zones. In the irrigated areas the two most important *kharif* crops are rice and cotton. In areas of high water table, heavy soils, and greater rainfall, rice tends to dominate, while in the drier areas cotton is generally planted. Thus, one major division is between areas suited to rice and areas suited to cotton. Since growing conditions vary significantly as one moves from north to south, there are four distinct cotton or rice zones: cotton/wheat Sind, cotton/wheat Punjab, rice/other Sind, and rice/wheat Punjab.[11]

There is one zone centered around Faisalabad in which conditions are suitable for a number of *kharif* crops, with no single crop dominating. This will be termed the "mixed zone." The *barani* areas are considered distinct because of their dependence on rainfall. Finally, the area close to the left bank of the Indus in the Punjab, which has relatively less-developed irrigation facilities and thus low cropping intensities, is considered a separate zone. This makes a total of nine zones. Five are in the Punjab: rice/wheat, cotton/wheat, mixed, *barani,* and low-intensity. Two are in the Sind: rice/other and cotton/wheat. Because of similarities in cropping patterns and climate, D. I. Khan District of North-West Frontier Province (NWFP) is included in the low-intensity zone of the Punjab, and Nasirabad District of Baluchistan is in the rice/other zone of the Sind. The remaining districts in NWFP and Baluchistan make up the final two zones. Districts included in each zone are listed in Table 1, and a map of the zones is presented in Figure 1. Although the other districts in NWFP and Baluchistan are not homogeneous agroclimatically, it is not worthwhile to disaggregate them since they compose only 6.3 percent and 1.2 percent of wheat production, respectively. The contribution of each of the nine zones to total wheat production over the last 18 years is presented in Table 2, along with the average yield for wheat during that period.

Government Policy Toward Wheat

The government of Pakistan has intervened in the wheat market for decades.[12] Wheat was rationed in the urban areas during World War II as an emergency measure; after the war, markets for most commodities were freed, but the government continued to ration wheat and sugar. The ration system was changed to a partial provisioning system in the 1960s, with the government supplying less than the normal household requirements at the subsidized, ration-shop price. Wheat flour was also available at considerably higher prices on the open market.

Until the mid-1960s, most of the wheat in the ration shops was received as food aid. Two events caused a major change in the system. First, the war with India at this time led to a halt in U.S. PL480 shipments to both countries, during a time when domestic supplies were scarce. Second, the beginnings of the "green revolution" in 1967 and 1968 caused the country to move close to self-sufficiency in wheat production. Thus, in 1968 the government procured a large proportion of the wheat crop for the first time.

---

[10] The zones used here are based on but are not identical to those used in the PARC/CIMMYT (1986) report.

[11] Sind, Punjab, North-West Frontier, and Baluchistan are the four provinces of Pakistan.

[12] See Alderman, Chaudhry, and Garcia 1988 for a fuller explanation of government policies toward wheat consumption, and Cornelisse and Naqvi 1984 for a fuller description of wheat marketing.

Table 1—Districts of Pakistan, by agroclimatic zone

Zone[a]	District
Rice/wheat Punjab	Sialkot
	Gujrat
	Gujranwala
	Sheikhupura
	Lahore/Kasur
Mixed Punjab	Sardogha/Khushab
	Jhang
	Faisalabad/T. T. Singh
	Okara[b]
Cotton/wheat Punjab	Sahiwal[b]
	Bahawalnagar
	Bahawalpur
	R. Y. Khan
	Multan/Vehari
Low-intensity Punjab	D. G. Khan/Rajanpur
	Muzaffagarh/Leiah
	Mianwali/Bhakkar
	D. I. Khan
Barani Punjab	Attock
	Jhelum
	Rawalpindi/Islamabad
Cotton/wheat Sind	Sukkur[b]
	Khairpur
	Nawabshah
	Hyderabad[b]
	Tharparkar
Rice/other Sind	Jacobabad
	Larkana
	Dadu
	Thatta
	Badin[b]
	Shikarpur[b]
	Nasirabad[b]
	Karachi[b]
Other NWFP except D. I. Khan	
Other Baluchistan except Nasirabad	

[a] Punjab, Sind, North-West Frontier Province (NWFP), and Baluchistan are the four provinces of Pakistan. Because of cropping and climate similarities, the D. I. Khan District of NWFP is included in the low-intensity zone of the Punjab and the Nasirabad District of Baluchistan is included in the rice/other zone of the Sind.
[b] These districts were divided or created after 1967/68.

Since 1973/74, procurement has averaged just under one-fourth of production, ranging from 13 to 36 percent of the crop (Table 3).[13] The government typically announces a procurement price at planting time; this price occasionally has been adjusted upward a month prior to harvest. There is an active private trade in wheat that is regulated but not controlled by the government.

Usually, farmers have been free to sell wheat to private agents or to the government procurement agency. Until recently, however, the law did not allow private agents to

---

[13] See Pinckney 1989 for an analysis of the determinants of procurement size.

Figure 1—Agroclimatic zones of Pakistan

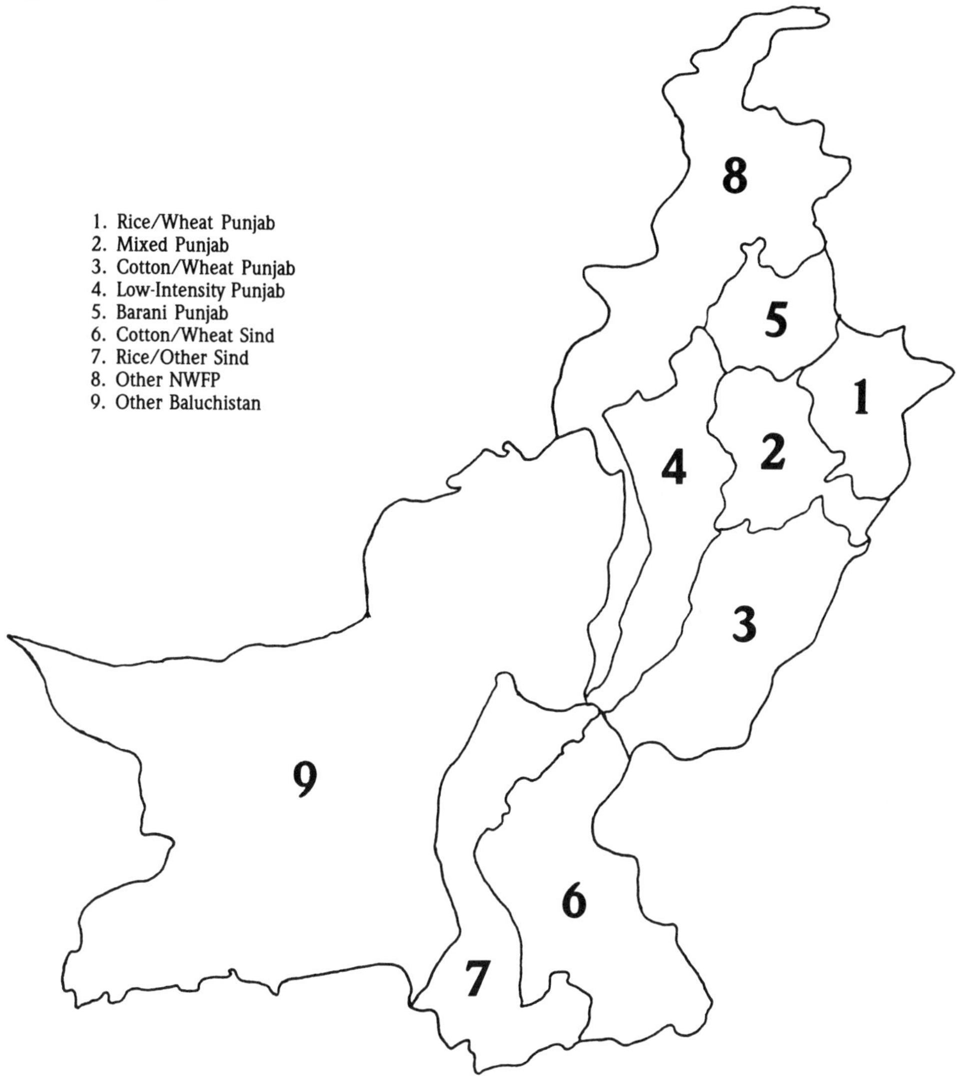

1. Rice/Wheat Punjab
2. Mixed Punjab
3. Cotton/Wheat Punjab
4. Low-Intensity Punjab
5. Barani Punjab
6. Cotton/Wheat Sind
7. Rice/Other Sind
8. Other NWFP
9. Other Baluchistan

Note: Punjab, Sind, North-West Frontier Province (NWFP), and Baluchistan are the four provinces of Pakistan.

transport wheat out of surplus areas during the harvest months. This law lowered the price in those zones and made the procurement price more attractive. In addition, there are allegations that in years of scarcity, particularly in the 1970s, some farmers were forced against their will to sell wheat to the government at the procurement price.

The relationship of the procurement price to the world price has gone through several stages.[14] From the late 1960s until the 1972 rise in world prices, the procurement price was higher than import parity at the official exchange rate. Such policies

---

[14] See Hamid et al. 1987 and Dorosh and Valdés 1989 for a discussion of these issues.

Table 2—Average shares and yields of Pakistan's wheat production, by agroclimatic zone

Zone[a]	Share, 1968 to 1985	Yield, 1981 to 1985
	(percent)	(metric tons/hectare)
Other Baluchistan	1.2	1.14
Barani Punjab	4.0	0.94
Rice/other Sind	4.3	1.56
Other NWFP	6.3	1.14
Low-intensity Punjab	10.2	1.29
Cotton/wheat Sind	12.8	2.16
Rice/wheat Punjab	16.5	1.53
Mixed Punjab	20.3	1.87
Cotton/wheat Punjab	24.3	1.83

Source: Pakistan, Ministry of Food, Agriculture, and Cooperatives, Food and Agriculture Division, *Agricultural Statistics of Pakistan* (Islamabad: Government Press, 1985).
[a] Baluchistan, Punjab, Sind, and North-West Frontier Province (NWFP) are the four provinces of Pakistan.

were possible since the government had (and continues to have) monopoly control of wheat imports and exports. From 1972 to 1976, the procurement price was lower than export parity; since that time, the procurement price has tracked export parity rather closely, moving to a level between import and export parity in 1986 and 1987. Since Pakistan has been approximately self-sufficient in wheat during the 1980s, the more recent price regime seems reasonable. When adjustments are made for exchange rate and trade policies, however, the recent procurement prices fall well short of export parity (see Dorosh and Valdés 1989).

On the consumption side, the government dismantled the partial provisioning system for sugar in 1983 and for wheat in 1987. To assure consumers that wheat flour prices will not skyrocket, the government guarantees that it will sell at a certain price all the wheat that is demanded. The implications of this system for procurement and government cost are examined in Chapter 5.

Table 3 presents the results of these policies on government procurement, offtake, imports, and stocks. There are clearly some data problems, since computed closing stocks (equal to opening stocks plus procurement plus net imports minus offtakes) fail to equal actual closing stocks. The problems are most likely with the stocks data, since different sources present conflicting numbers. Nevertheless, it is clear that interannual stockholding has increased in recent years. The costs of such a policy, and possible methods for lowering these costs, are examined in subsequent chapters.

Supply Responsiveness of Wheat

Relative prices play an important role in the allocation of resources within agriculture and between agriculture and nonagriculture. This section attempts to measure the responsiveness of wheat production to relative price changes. Since the specific cropping pattern would be expected to have an effect on price responsiveness, equations are estimated by zone, with the total supply response an aggregation of the zonal estimates.

Linear equations for both yields and areas are estimated for each zone. Estimated equations are given in Appendix 1 (Tables 27 and 28) and results are reported in detail in Pinckney 1989. Table 4 presents the implied elasticities at the mean.

Table 3—Wheat production, stocks, procurement, offtake, and imports, 1970/71-1986/87

Year	Production from Previous Year	Opening Stocks	Procurement	Offtake	Net Imports	Computed Closing Stocks	Actual Closing Stocks
				(1,000 metric tons)			
1970/71	7,294	33	1,017	1,196	269	123	165
1971/72	6,476	165	841	1,323	439	122	42
1972/73	6,890	42	265	1,588	1,418	137	132
1973/74	7,442	132	1,292	2,210	1,079	293	75
1974/75	7,629	75	1,265	2,296	1,173	217	75
1975/76	7,673	75	1,333	2,322	1,273	359	389
1976/77	8,691	389	2,252	2,759	505	387	440
1977/78	9,144	440	1,850	2,880	822	232	85
1978/79	8,367	85	1,093	2,977	2,112	313	236
1979/80	9,950	236	2,402	2,744	668	562	632
1980/81	10,587	632	3,043	2,768	20	927	997
1981/82	11,476	997	3,926	3,214	101	1,810	1,727
1982/83	11,304	1,727	3,132	3,115	−53	1,691	1,702
1983/84	12,414	1,702	3,826	3,251	−191	2,086	1,855
1984/85	10,882	1,855	2,505	3,695	544	1,209	1,047
1985/86	11,703	1,047	2,487	3,477	1,482	1,539	1,258
1986/87	13,940	1,258	5,073	3,648	80	2,763	2,876

Sources: Data originate from provincial food departments, but were collected from the Ministry of Food, Agriculture, and Cooperatives, Islamabad; also, Pakistan, Ministry of Food, Agriculture, and Cooperatives, Planning Unit, Early Warning System Project, *Wheat Situation Report,* various issues (Islamabad: Government Press, various years).

Notes: Opening stocks are given as of May 1. Procurement, offtake, and imports are summed from May 1 to April 30. Since procurement in the Sind begins in April, some of the wheat included in the procurement statistics actually is from the next year's crop. This also causes the procurement statistics in this table to differ from most other series, which are usually given for April-March. It would have been preferable to present all series for April-March; however, stocks for the Pakistan Agricultural Supply and Storage Corporation (PASSCO) are only available for May 1 of some years, and offtake in Azad Kashmir and net imports are only available on an annual, May-April basis for most years. Computed closing stocks are calculated as opening stocks plus procurement and net imports, minus offtake.

In some of the area equations, expected gross revenue from wheat production is used rather than the price of wheat. If expected yields are not changing, the effect of an increase in price is interpreted as if the parameter were estimated with the price of wheat. Using expected revenue makes for more accurate estimation if relative yields have been changing rapidly over time.

Area exhibits a wide range of response values to the price of wheat. The weighted average area elasticity for all Pakistan is 0.09 in the short run, about 0.20 in the long run. The highest short-run response was for other Baluchistan at 0.31, while the two Sind zones have negative area response to price (neither of these is significantly different from zero). Yield responses are much closer together; most of the results are between 0.29 and 0.57. The weighted average for all Pakistan is 0.34, implying a total short-run response to price of 0.43 (area plus yield). This is fairly high for a staple crop in a less-developed country.

The price of fertilizer has a negative effect on area in several zones, as the weighted average of all zones is −0.06. Cotton had the only cross price to affect wheat production significantly in these equations, with significant negative effects on yields in the two cotton/wheat zones. This is reasonable, since wheat is planted after cotton, and a higher cotton price increases the incentive to leave the crop in the ground longer. This delays wheat planting past the optimal date, however, thus decreasing wheat yields.

Table 4—Wheat supply elasticities with respect to prices, by agroclimatic zone

| | Own Price | | | Fertilizer Price, Area | Cotton Price, Yield |
| | Area | | | | |
Zone[a]	Short Run	Long Run	Yield		
Rice/wheat Punjab	0.25***	0.39***	0.57*	. . .	. . .
Mixed Punjab	0.04	0.21	0.43**	−0.09**	. . .
Cotton/wheat Punjab	0.03	0.11	0.29**	−0.06	−0.14**
Low-intensity Punjab	0.16*	0.32*	0.57*	−0.11	. . .
Barani Punjab	0.21***	0.31***	0.15***	. . .	. . .
Rice/other Sind	−0.02	−0.04	0.41	−0.11	. . .
Cotton/wheat Sind	−0.04	−0.04	−0.07	−0.12*	−0.08**
Other NWFP	0.20**	0.38**	0.33	. . .	. . .
Other Baluchistan	0.31***	0.40***	0.08	0.25	. . .
All Pakistan[b]	0.09	0.20	0.34	−0.06	−0.04
All Pakistan[b]	0.08	0.14	0.32	−0.03	−0.04

Note: All area elasticities, except those for *barani* Punjab and rice/other Sind, were estimated with *expected revenue* instead of price.
[a] Punjab, Sind, North-West Frontier Province (NWFP), and Baluchistan are the four provinces of Pakistan.
[b] The first "All Pakistan" line presents weighted averages of the elasticities for the individual zones. The second "All Pakistan" line also presents weighted averages, but in this case all elasticities not significantly different from zero at the 90 percent level are assumed to equal zero.
* Denotes 90 percent confidence level.
** Denotes 95 percent confidence level.
***Denotes 99 percent confidence level.

There was an insignificant positive effect of cotton price on wheat area, which may result from some farmers increasing their wheat area to meet subsistence needs when they know that late planting due to additional cotton picking will reduce their wheat yields.

Trends in Wheat Production

As shown in Figure 2, Pakistan's wheat production has increased rapidly, with a particularly large jump in the 1967/68 crop year. Because of the dramatic discontinuity in trend in that year, all estimates are made beginning in 1967/68. Both linear and exponential trends are reported in Table 5. Appendix 2 describes the method used to compare the fit of the linear and exponential equations.

With the exception of the small negative trend in area planted in the *barani* Punjab, all trends of both area and yield are positive. In all cases area trends are exponential and in most cases yield trends are linear. Yield trends in both the *barani* Punjab and other Baluchistan zone have been experiencing exponential growth.

The cotton/wheat zones in the Punjab and the Sind have the highest growth rates in area among the zones. This is as much due to an increase in double cropping as to increases in area. Normally, an increase in cropping intensity would be expected to be associated with a decline in yields. This holds true in the cotton/wheat Punjab, since historical yield increases are the second lowest of all the zones, but the cotton/wheat Sind has the highest linear trend in yields.

Projecting the national trends to the year 2000 leads to production of 19.9 million tons; the trends by zone lead to the higher figure of 20.9 million tons because of the exponential yields in two zones. These projections are based only on history, however, with no consideration of future constraints on production. There is a variety of reasons for believing that future growth in total area planted will not increase at the historical

24

Figure 2—Wheat production in Pakistan, 1956-85

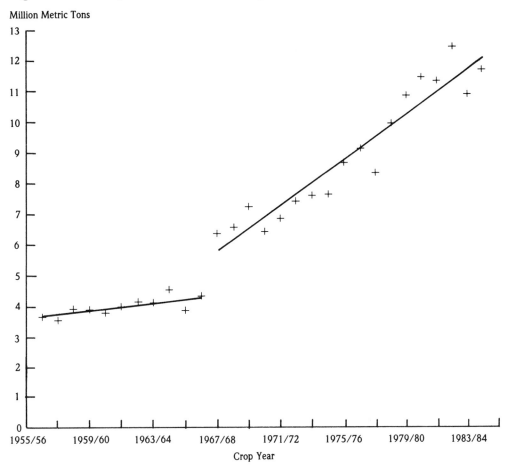

Million Metric Tons

Crop Year

Source: Pakistan, Ministry of Food, Agriculture, and Cooperatives, Food and Agriculture Division, *Agricultural Statistics of Pakistan* (Islamabad: Government Press, 1985).

rate (Hamid et al. 1987). Even fairly optimistic assumptions show water availability between 1985 and 2000 increasing at less than half of the rate at which it expanded between 1968 and 1985. Since water availability is the primary constraint on cropped area, an overall growth of cropped area at 0.8 percent per year—only about half of the historical rate—is reasonable. Historically, wheat area as a percentage of total cropped area has been close to constant. Thus, future growth in wheat area is expected to grow at about 0.8 percent per year.

The primary impetus behind the historical increase in wheat yields has been the switch from traditional to high-yielding varieties (HYVs). This change is virtually complete, with the major wheat-producing areas now planting more than 95 percent of their land in HYVs. Thus, future yield growth depends on increases in the yields of HYVs. The national trend in yields of HYVs from 1968 to 1985 is only 0.9 percent annually, much less than the 2.7 percent overall trend reported in Table 5. Nevertheless, wheat yields are expected to grow at the historic *linear* trend. The linear trend may

25

Table 5—Linear and exponential trend growth rates for wheat area and yield, by zone

Zone[a]	Area		Yield	
	Linear Trend	Exponential Trend	Linear Trend	Exponential Trend
	(1,000 hectares)	(percent)	(kilograms/hectare)	(percent)
Rice/wheat Punjab	11.7	1.0[b]	40[b]	3.2
	(1.6)	(0.1)	(6.0)	(0.4)
Mixed Punjab	8.7	0.8[b]	25[b]	1.5
	(1.7)	(0.2)	(5.0)	(0.3)
Cotton/wheat Punjab	30.5	2.3[b]	23[b]	1.4
	(3.4)	(0.3)	(4.0)	(0.2)
Low-intensity Punjab	12.4	1.6[b]	21[b]	1.8
	(1.6)	(0.2)	(5.0)	(0.4)
Barani Punjab	−0.9	−0.2[b]	37	5.7[b]
	(0.8)	(0.1)	(6.0)	(0.8)
Rice/other Sind	2.8	0.9[b]	50[b]	4.2
	(1.6)	(0.6)	(4.0)	(0.4)
Cotton/wheat Sind	15.1	2.2[b]	66[b]	4.0
	(2.1)	(0.3)	(4.0)	(0.3)
Other NWFP	11.7	1.9[b]	37[b]	4.3
	(1.3)	(0.2)	(3.0)	(0.4)
Other Baluchistan	1.4	0.9[b]	49	6.5[b]
	(1.2)	(0.9)	(7.0)	(1.2)
All Pakistan	93.4	1.4[b]	36[b]	2.7
	(12.1)	(0.2)	(3.0)	(0.2)

Source: Author's estimates based on data from Pakistan, Ministry of Food, Agriculture, and Cooperatives, Food and Agriculture Division, *Agricultural Statistics of Pakistan* (Islamabad: Government Press, 1985).
Note: The figures in parentheses are the standard errors.
[a] Punjab, Sind, North-West Frontier Province (NWFP), and Baluchistan are the four provinces of Pakistan.
[b] This trend is the best fit.

have been the best fit because the constraints in recent years are beginning to become apparent statistically. The linear yield trend, together with the area assumption, leads to an estimate of wheat production in the year 2000 of 17.8 million tons.

Changes in Wheat Consumption

Historical data on wheat consumption are not as readily available as data on production. The most detailed data are those contained in the Household Income and Expenditure Surveys (HIESs). In addition, annual estimates of consumption per capita can be derived through the food balance approach; that is, taking annual production of wheat, subtracting losses and government procurement, adding government offtakes, and dividing by the population. Both HIES data and food balance estimates are presented in Table 6.

Both the survey data and the food balance estimates move up and down from year to year, with no clear trend, particularly if the suspiciously low 1971/72 food balance figure is ignored. As is usual in such comparisons, the surveys estimate average per capita consumption 8-27 percent higher than food balance sheet data.

Table 6—Estimates of annual per capita wheat consumption, 1970/71-1986/87

Year	Rural	Urban	Average	Food Balance	Percent Difference
			(kilograms/year)		
1970/71	...	...	...	110	...
1971/72	139	119	134	98	−27
1972/73	...	...	...	115	...
1973/74	...	...	...	112	...
1974/75	...	...	...	113	...
1975/76	...	...	...	112	...
1976/77	...	...	...	112	...
1977/78	...	...	...	122	...
1978/79	147	115	138	120	−13
1979/80	...	...	...	115	...
1980/81	...	...	...	115	...
1981/82	150	100	136	111	−18
1982/83	...	...	...	115	...
1983/84	...	...	...	116	...
1984/85	139	105	129	119	−8
1985/86	...	...	...	118	...
1986/87	...	...	...	111	...

Sources: Data for 1971/72, 1978/79, and 1984/85 are from Pakistan, Federal Bureau of Statistics, *Household Income and Expenditure Survey* (Islamabad: Government Press, 1971/72, 1979, and 1984/85); data for 1981/82 are from Peter A. Cornelisse and Syed N. H. Naqvi, *The Anatomy of the Wheat Market in Pakistan* (Rotterdam: Erasmus University, and Islamabad: Pakistan Institute for Development Economics, 1984).

In some countries, the shift of the population from rural to urban areas could be expected to induce a shift in consumption patterns. In such a case, projections of demand should include an urbanization variable. Since Table 6 shows that urban wheat consumption is considerably lower than rural wheat consumption, such a consideration may appear to be important for Pakistan. Most analysts in Pakistan, however, attribute the difference in urban and rural consumption patterns to ethnic differences. At the time of partition, a large number of rice-eating Moslems migrated to Pakistan's cities from present-day India. Ever since, average wheat consumption has been lower and average rice consumption higher in the cities, but a wheat-eating Pakistani who migrates from the rural to the urban areas is not expected to shift from wheat to rice. Thus, urbanization does not enter the equation for the projection of consumption.

For purposes of projecting per capita consumption into the future, it is useful to estimate income elasticities and expected increases in income separately. Cross-sectional estimates of income elasticities for wheat from the 1979 HIESs yield 0.11 and 0.21 (derived from Cheema and Malik 1985 and Ahmed, Leung, and Stern 1986). Although time series estimates of income elasticities can differ significantly from cross-sectional estimates, in this case the time series estimate based on 1968-84 data yields an elasticity of 0.19. Thus the income elasticity of wheat appears to be small but positive.

A constant-price demand projection for wheat can be produced by combining the income elasticity with projections of population and income per capita. The historical annual growth in real GDP over the last 25 years has averaged 5.6 percent. This is assumed for future growth, with income per capita calculated by subtracting the population growth rate. In order to project population, an assumption needs to be made about the Afghan refugees. About 1.8 million refugees are assumed to stay in Pakistan. The population growth rate is projected to be constant at 3.1 percent annually until

1990, then to decline steadily to 2.6 percent by the year 2000. Together these assumptions imply that Pakistan's population will grow to 149 million by 2000. These numbers, combined with the income elasticity of 0.19, yield a constant-price demand for wheat of 19.1 million tons in 2000.

Balancing Supply and Demand

After allowing for a 10 percent reduction in the projected supply for seed, feed, and waste, 16.0 million tons are available for domestic consumption versus a demand of 19.1 million tons. This gap could be closed through trade or price increases. A rough estimate of the implied price change can be calculated by solving constant elasticity demand and supply curves using the long-term supply elasticity of 0.46 (the sum of the area and yield elasticities in the bottom row of Table 4) and a representative demand elasticity for a staple food of −0.25.

These numbers imply that a price rise of about 28 percent would balance supply and demand in the year 2000 at about 18 million tons consumed, or 20 million tons produced before the seed, feed, and waste reduction. This implies an average annual growth in wheat production of about 3.3 percent. The procurement price would rise to about 102 1985 rupees (Rs) per 40 kilograms from its 1985 level of Rs80, and there would be a corresponding rise in the release price.[15] This would still be below the import parity price unless world wheat prices were to fall precipitously. Per capita consumption actually rises slightly from its 1985 base under these assumptions to about 121 kilograms per year. The price rise thus serves primarily to cancel out the increase in consumption that would have resulted, all else remaining the same, from the increase in per capita income.[16]

Hamid et al. (1987) examine the effects of trends on 11 different crops, and use theoretically consistent matrices of supply and demand elasticities and different assumptions about trade policy to balance supply and demand by allowing prices to change, taking into account both own- and cross-price effects. The base case makes the same assumptions about trends as the single-market model in the previous paragraph. The interactions among commodities, however, result in wheat prices rising to Rs106 per 40 kilograms in 1985 rupees by the year 2000. Since this price is below import parity, production and per capita consumption of wheat adjust to the price rise and balance without exports or imports taking place. Production and consumption end up rising at 3.3 percent per year from 1985. Hamid et al. consider several other scenarios about world prices and trade policies, but wheat production and consumption in 1999/2000 do not vary from the base case by more than 2.0 percent.

Thus, in the remainder of this study it is assumed that wheat production and consumption will grow at about 3.3 percent per year in the medium term. In addition, Pakistan is expected to remain self-sufficient in a normal production year at prices between import and export parity. It is this situation that raises the possibility of holding interannual supply stabilization stocks. In order to conduct that analysis, it is necessary first to examine the historical pattern of instability in supply.

---

[15] At the 1985 average exchange rate of about Rs16 per U.S. dollar, Rs80 per 40 kilograms is US$125 per ton.
[16] Alderman (1988a) has estimated a demand system that leads to a surprisingly high own-price demand elasticity for wheat of −0.96 in the rural areas and −0.34 in the urban areas. These higher numbers would lessen the price increase required to balance supply and demand, but would lower per capita consumption below its 1985 level.

Instability of Pakistan's Wheat Production

Instability is often measured in terms of the coefficient of variation of production—that is, the standard deviation of production divided by the mean, expressed as a percentage. A high coefficient of variation implies high instability relative to the average size of the crop, leading to increased fiscal costs for the same degree of price stability. The absolute level of instability is given by the standard deviation.

One simple method for measuring both the level of instability and its trend is to compute the coefficient of variation for detrended production data for successive 10-year periods. This is done for wheat at the national level in Table 7. The table is created in the following manner. A linear trend is calculated for area, yield, and production for each of the commodities for the entire time period. The standard deviation of the residuals from these regressions is then computed for each successive 10-year interval and divided by average production for that period to yield the coefficient of variation of the detrended series.

Table 7 shows that wheat production instability has been increasing over time, as the increase in yield instability has more than offset the decline in area instability. The coefficient of variation of production has increased from 4.8 to 7.8 percent from 1968-77 to 1978-87 even though the coefficient of variation for area has decreased from 4.6 to 2.1 percent. Yield instability more than doubles, from 3.3 to 6.7 percent, although much of the increase occurred in the first year.

Increases in total variability result from a combination of statistical factors. Hazell (1982, 1984) has developed a technique for decomposing the variance of crop production into component parts. Hazell (1984) explains the methodology in detail. This technique has been especially useful for identifying whether or not production variance has been changing over time and, if so, discovering the source of the change. In most of the countries studied to date, the variance of cereal production has been increasing.

Hazell (1988) presents basic results for numerous countries, including Pakistan. These results are informative because of the comparison across countries that they allow. Interestingly, the coefficient of variation of production of cereals in Pakistan for

Table 7—Changes in the means and variability of wheat production in Pakistan, 1968-87

Year	Mean			Coefficient of Variation		
	Production	Area	Yield	Production	Area	Yield
	(1,000 metric tons)	(1,000 hectares)	(metric tons/ hectare)	(percent)		
1968-77	7,420	6,054	1.23	4.8	4.6	3.3
1969-78	7,616	6,092	1.25	5.5	4.3	4.1
1970-79	7,949	6,145	1.29	5.4	3.5	4.1
1971-80	8,305	6,214	1.33	5.7	2.8	4.2
1972-81	8,805	6,315	1.39	6.4	2.9	4.2
1973-82	9,257	6,457	1.43	6.0	3.3	4.0
1974-83	9,754	6,600	1.47	6.4	3.7	4.0
1975-84	10,080	6,723	1.49	7.0	3.7	5.4
1976-85	10,483	6,868	1.52	6.8	2.8	5.5
1977-86	11,013	6,997	1.57	6.9	2.2	6.1
1978-87	11,310	7,114	1.59	7.8	2.1	6.7

Source: Author's calculations based on data from Pakistan, Ministry of Food, Agriculture, and Cooperatives, Food and Agriculture Division, *Agricultural Statistics of Pakistan* (Islamabad: Government Press, 1985).

1972-83 is the second smallest of the 34 countries in the study. Although Table 7 shows some increase in instability since 1983, it is important to note that Pakistan's problems in this regard are far fewer than those for almost any other country in the world, primarily because of the prevalence of irrigation.

The results of Hazell's study are expanded here for Pakistan by extending the time period to 1984/85, considering only the post-green revolution period, and by using agro-ecological zone data. Two decompositions are carried out here. First, the variance of wheat production for the entire period is decomposed by production zone. Second, the change in the variance from the first half to the second half of the post-green revolution period is decomposed by production zone.

Table 8 presents the results of decomposing the total variance of wheat production by agroclimatic zone. The results are dominated by the correlations of wheat production among zones, as more than 76 percent of the variance can be attributed to these correlations. Nevertheless, it is interesting that of the remaining 24 percent of the variance, the rice/wheat Punjab zone accounts for a disproportionately high share. This zone produces about 16 percent of the country's wheat, but is responsible for over 25 percent of the variance attributable to individual zones. Cotton/wheat Sind, on the other hand, contributes less to total variance than its proportion of production.

A priori, one might expect the rainfed *(barani)* areas to be responsible for a large share of the variance, but this view is not supported by the analysis. The *barani* Punjab zone is responsible for only 5.5 percent of the zone-specific variance—higher than its share of wheat production, but small in total. Even if all the variance of other Baluchistan and other NWFP is added to the *barani* Punjab variance, the total is less than 10.0 percent. The figure of 10.0 percent overstates the rainfed areas' contribution to total variance, since both NWFP and Baluchistan grow some irrigated wheat.

In order to examine two contrasting zones, changes in the mean and variability of wheat production in the rice/wheat Punjab and the cotton/wheat Sind zones are

Table 8—A decomposition of the total variance of wheat production, 1967/68-1984/85

Zone[a]	Percent of Variance	Percent of Variance Directly Attributable to Zones	Percent of Production
Rice/wheat Punjab	6.0	25.6	16.5
Mixed Punjab	3.9	16.5	20.2
Cotton/wheat Punjab	6.7	28.5	24.3
Low-intensity Punjab	1.5	6.4	10.2
Barani Punjab	1.3	5.5	3.9
Rice/other Sind	0.5	2.3	4.3
Cotton/wheat Sind	2.4	10.1	13.0
Other NWFP	0.9	4.0	6.4
Other Baluchistan	0.3	1.1	1.2
Subtotal	23.5	. . .	. . .
Interzone covariances	76.5	. . .	. . .
Total	100.0	100.0	100.0

Source: Author's calculations based on data from Pakistan, Ministry of Food, Agriculture, and Cooperatives, Food and Agriculture Division, *Agricultural Statistics of Pakistan* (Islamabad: Government Press, 1985).

Note: Parts may not add to totals because of rounding.

[a] Punjab, Sind, North-West Frontier Province (NWFP), and Baluchistan are the four provinces of Pakistan.

presented in Tables 9 and 10. Rice/wheat Punjab exhibits a large increase in production variability over time, all of which is attributable to an increase in yield variability. The cotton/wheat Sind zone, on the other hand, shows declining variability of both areas and yields. Overall variability is higher in cotton/wheat Sind at the beginning of the period, but by the end of the period yield variability in this zone is only 40 percent of yield variability in rice/wheat Punjab, more than offsetting the continued lower area variability in rice/wheat Punjab. A partial explanation for the rice/wheat Punjab increase in variability is that this zone was the hardest hit during the 1978 blight attack.

The variance decomposition approach can also be used to study changes in variability of wheat production more rigorously than the moving-average, coefficient-of-variation approach. For this purpose, the time period is divided into two segments of equal length: 1967/68-1975/76 and 1976/77-1984/85. The variance of the detrended series for each period is then computed.

Table 9—Changes in the mean and variability of wheat production, rice/wheat Punjab zone, 1968-85

Years	Mean			Coefficient of Variation		
	Production	Area	Yield	Production	Area	Yield
	(1,000 metric tons)	(1,000 hectares)	(metric tons/ hectare)	(percent)		
1968-77	1,233	1,073	1.15	6.4	3.0	6.4
1969-78	1,276	1,085	1.18	7.7	2.9	7.2
1970-79	1,345	1,088	1.23	7.9	2.0	7.4
1971-80	1,422	1,100	1.29	9.2	2.0	8.3
1972-81	1,513	1,109	1.36	9.8	1.8	8.7
1973-82	1,572	1,129	1.39	9.5	2.4	9.5
1974-83	1,653	1,146	1.44	9.3	2.8	9.0
1975-84	1,699	1,157	1.46	10.2	2.8	9.9
1976-85	1,751	1,171	1.49	10.3	2.5	10.2

Source: Author's calculations based on data from Pakistan, Ministry of Food, Agriculture, and Cooperatives, Food and Agriculture Division, *Agricultural Statistics of Pakistan* (Islamabad: Government Press, 1985).

Table 10—Changes in the mean and variability of wheat production, cotton/wheat Sind zone, 1968-85

Years	Mean			Coefficient of Variation		
	Production	Area	Yield	Production	Area	Yield
	(1,000 metric tons)	(1,000 hectares)	(metric tons/ hectare)	(percent)		
1968-77	864	593	1.46	8.4	8.0	6.1
1969-78	912	601	1.52	8.5	7.4	6.2
1970-79	981	616	1.59	7.8	7.5	5.5
1971-80	1,040	628	1.65	6.8	6.6	5.2
1972-81	1,110	645	1.70	6.7	6.8	4.4
1973-82	1,195	668	1.77	7.4	6.9	4.2
1974-83	1,284	690	1.84	7.2	6.5	4.4
1975-84	1,352	708	1.89	7.4	6.3	4.3
1976-85	1,440	730	1.95	6.8	5.2	4.2

Source: Author's calculations based on data from Pakistan, Ministry of Food, Agriculture, and Cooperatives, Food and Agriculture Division, *Agricultural Statistics of Pakistan* (Islamabad: Government Press, 1985).

Table 11 provides a breakdown of the change in the variance of wheat production by agroclimatic zone. Because of the high correlations between production fluctuations in the different zones, only 17 percent of the change in variance can be attributed directly to the different zones. However, rice/wheat Punjab is responsible for 40 percent of this change, even though that zone accounts for only 17 percent of the increase in total production. In contrast, the cotton/wheat Sind zone is responsible for only 3 percent of the change in variance but contributed 19 percent of the increase in production.

Thus, in Pakistan the variability of wheat production has been increasing over time, while the variability of most other cereals has been declining. This is in contrast to Hazell's (1988) finding that wheat production in most countries is becoming more stable over time. The increase in the coefficient of variation of wheat production, however, is not statistically significant.

In the analysis that follows, it is necessary to use a parameter for the inherent instability of wheat production, that is, the degree to which wheat production would fluctuate if government policy were constant. The historical degree of variability should be an overestimate of this number, since past changes in government pricing and marketing policies most likely have caused some of the observed production fluctuations. Estimates of yield variability should be closer to the purely random effect than production variability, although government policies could affect yields through their impact on the use of variable inputs such as fertilizer, and random weather events can affect harvested areas, particularly in *barani* zones, by causing a planted field to be abandoned.

Table 7 shows that the coefficients of variation of wheat yield and production are 6.7 percent and 7.8 percent, respectively, for the most recent 10-year period. Both of these figures are the highest for their series. Since the proper number to use for the inherent instability of production should be somewhat less than actual past yield instability, a figure of 6.0 percent is used here. Sensitivity analysis is included for a value of 7.0 percent. These assumptions should be on the high side, for as recently as 1974-83 the coefficient of variation was only 4.0 percent for yields. Consequently, the results below should be slightly biased toward high costs and high optimal stock levels. This bias should cover the relatively small degree of instability added by other cereals.

In sum, this section has shown that Pakistan's variability of cereal production is lower than that of most countries, although it has been increasing somewhat over time. Increases in variability in the Punjab—particularly in the rice/wheat Punjab zone—account for most of the increase in wheat variability. Chapter 4 examines how the government can use price, trade, and storage policy to stabilize consumption and prices in the face of these fluctuations in production.

Table 11—A decomposition of the change in variance of wheat production, 1967/68-1975/76 to 1976/77-1984/85

Zone[a]	Source of Change					Row Sum	Share of Variance Attributable Directly to Zones	Zonal Share of Increase in Production
	Change in Mean Yield	Change in Mean Area	Change in Yield Variance and Covariance	Change in Area Variance and Covariance	Area-Yield Covariance, Interaction Terms, and Residual			
	(percent)							
Rice/wheat Punjab	0.20	0.26	4.42	-0.02	1.87	6.73	39.76	16.8
Mixed Punjab	0.10	0.28	0.66	-0.18	0.64	1.49	8.83	10.7
Cotton/wheat Punjab	0.50	0.41	2.49	-0.72	2.18	4.86	28.73	23.2
Low-intensity Punjab	0.02	0.11	0.61	-0.05	1.01	1.70	10.05	8.0
Barani Punjab	0.06	0.00	1.26	0.00	0.24	1.56	9.21	5.6
Rice/other Sind	0.33	0.04	-0.06	-0.20	-0.20	-0.10	-0.58	5.8
Cotton/wheat Sind	0.86	0.32	0.09	-0.65	-0.05	0.57	3.40	19.0
Other NWFP	0.18	0.18	-0.25	0.01	-0.05	0.08	0.45	8.8
Other Baluchistan	0.03	0.02	-0.09	0.00	0.06	0.03	0.15	2.2
Total variance within zones	2.29	1.61	9.12	-1.81	5.71	16.91	100.00	...
Interzone covariances	7.36	2.51	33.40	-3.82	43.62	83.08	...	...
Column sums	9.65	4.13	42.52	-5.63	49.33	100.00	...	...

Source: Author's calculations based on data from Pakistan, Ministry of Food, Agriculture, and Cooperatives, Food and Agriculture Division, *Agricultural Statistics of Pakistan* (Islamabad: Government Press, 1985).

Note: Parts may not add to totals because of rounding.

[a] Punjab, Sind, North-West Frontier Province (NWFP), and Baluchistan are the four provinces of Pakistan.

33

4

THE DEMAND FOR INTERANNUAL SUPPLY STABILIZATION STOCKS

The most commonly heard justification for the creation of additional government storage space is the need to stabilize price and supply across surplus and deficit years. This chapter examines the rationale for holding interannual supply stabilization stocks in Pakistan. An optimization model is used to examine questions about the appropriate role of foreign trade and stockholding given the inherent instability of the production system and the government's objectives of stabilizing prices without committing an inordinate percentage of its fiscal resources. Another consideration is whether or not it is worthwhile for Pakistan to build additional storage to accommodate the interannual supply stabilization stocks that are efficient to hold. Policy modifications to make the system more efficient are investigated; for example, adjusting the domestic purchasing price to changes in the world price and to changes in domestic production. The value of such policy modifications is measured, and a scenario to show how these policies might work in practice is presented.

Efficient Policy Design for Price Stabilization

This section explores the elements of an efficient supply stabilization policy from the government's perspective. To present government officials with choices that are meaningful to them, it is necessary to take their objectives into consideration. Governments have multiple objectives in supply stabilization policy. Two of the most important will be considered here: minimizing price and consumption variability, and minimizing fiscal expenditure.[17] The price stability goal as defined here is concerned with the prevailing price paid for the staple food. Price rather than consumption is the stated goal, since price is observable but consumption is not. The government is assumed to stand ready to buy or sell sufficient quantities to enforce its price on both official and private markets, importing the quantities if necessary.

The assumed link between consumption stability and price stability implies that income and cross-price effects on wheat consumption are relatively minor. The predominance of wheat in calorie consumption ensures that cross-price effects from other markets on wheat consumption are small. The importance of income fluctuations on wheat demand can be estimated from past data. The coefficient of variation of detrended per capita income from 1971/72 to 1984/85 is 1.5 percent. Assuming an income elasticity for wheat of about 0.2, as discussed in Chapter 3, this implies that the coefficient of variation of wheat demand resulting from income fluctuations is only 0.3 percent. This is totally dwarfed by the 6.0-7.0 percent figure for the coefficient of

---

[17] In some countries, minimizing imports is a separate objective beyond minimizing cost. This is the case when the international market for the staple food is quite thin and thus supplies may not be available (rice, white maize) or when the closest commodity substitute for the domestic staple is considered inferior by the population (yellow maize for white maize). See Pinckney 1988b for a supply stabilization study with three government objectives.

variation of supply. Consequently, little information would be added to the results by distinguishing between consumption and price variability.[18]

Economists have debated whether or not price stability is welfare-enhancing (Waugh 1944; Oi 1961; Massell 1969; Samuelson 1972; Wright and Williams 1988). For the purposes at hand, that debate is irrelevant. With varying degrees of success, most governments have attempted to control prices for decades and will continue to do so. There is no question that governments—including the government of Pakistan—perceive it to be in the interest of the country and the government to stabilize prices. The question then becomes, What is the trade-off between price stability and fiscal cost, and how can a simple and efficient policy be designed to achieve the best possible combination of outcomes for those two objectives? Government justification of the price stability objective usually emphasizes the large short-run costs to poor consumers of high prices; these costs, rather than a consumer-surplus measure, are calculated below to give some indication of the costs of price variability.

The study is concerned with government control of the *variability* of prices rather than the *level* of prices. For this reason, the analysis in this chapter assumes that the government has a target price and considers how prices should vary from that target from year to year given government objectives and unanticipated changes in production and world price. Although in the model the target is assumed to be the price that clears the domestic market with no foreign trade when production is normal, results are not particularly sensitive to the choice of target within a reasonable range. Readers interested in an analysis of the appropriate level of prices can refer to other works, notably Dorosh and Valdés 1989. The remainder of this chapter shows clearly that the analysis of the appropriate amount of price variability is complex enough to stand on its own, without an analysis of price level.

Methodology

A simple, single-market model is used to characterize the wheat sector of Pakistan. As the advantages and disadvantages of this methodology have been discussed at length elsewhere (Pinckney 1988b), only a brief overview of the model is presented here. A fuller description is provided in Appendix 3.

This is an open-economy model, but the government is assumed to control all imports and exports. Thus, supply available to the population in this annual model is equal to the sum of opening private stocks, government sales or offtake, and stochastic production:

$$S_t = PS_t + O_t + Q_t, \tag{4}$$

where

S_t = supply,
PS_t = opening private stocks (held by all parties, including households),

---

[18] A reviewer suggests that, since wheat production fluctuations are in the model, income fluctuations resulting from these supply fluctuations could be included. Again, the effect is so small that it can be ignored. Wheat production accounts for about 7.5 percent of value added in Pakistan's economy. Assuming that the coefficient of variation of value added equals that for production (it actually will be somewhat smaller, since prices will be inversely related to production), the coefficient of variation of per capita income that results from production fluctuations is 0.5 percent. The coefficient of variation of wheat demand thus would be 0.2 times 0.5, or 0.1 percent, a negligible amount.

O_t = offtake from government stocks, and

Q_t = production harvested during the time period.

Supply must be apportioned between carryout private stocks, PS_{t+1}, consumption, C_t, and government procurement, PC_t:

$$S_t = PS_{t+1} + C_t + PC_t. \tag{5}$$

Setting these equations equal and solving for consumption yields

$$C_t = (PS_t - PS_{t+1}) + (O_t - PC_t) + Q_t. \tag{6}$$

That is, consumption equals the net change in private stocks plus net offtake from government stocks plus production. For simplicity, it is assumed that

$$PS_t = PS_{t+1}. \tag{7}$$

Changes in private stocks at the end of the market year should be relatively small if the government succeeds in stabilizing interannual prices significantly. In Chapter 5 it is necessary to relax this assumption to study interseasonal prices.

With this assumption, equation (6) can be stated as

$$C_t = Q_t - NP_t. \tag{8}$$

That is, consumption equals production less net government procurement, NP. The net procurement variable is useful in an annual model. In any one year, the government both buys and sells grain for seasonal stabilization. The variable that buffers production fluctuations and thus affects the average annual price, however, is procurement net of offtakes. Thus, for the annual model, procurement and offtake can be collapsed into one variable. This is not possible in the seasonal model of Chapter 5.

Consumption is also a function of price, P_t:

$$C_t = f(P_t). \tag{9}$$

Supply balance on the government account implies that net procurement plus opening government stocks, GS_t, plus imports, M_t, must equal closing stocks plus exports, X_t:

$$NP_t + GS_t + M_t = GS_{t+1} + X_t. \tag{10}$$

Fiscal cost, FC, is a function of opening stocks, net procurement, imports, exports, the domestic price, and the world price, WP_t:

$$FC_t = g_1(GS_t, NP_t, M_t, X_t, P_t, WP_t). \tag{11}$$

Price variability, PV, is a function of the domestic price and the target price, P^*:

$$PV_t = g_2(P_t, P^*). \tag{12}$$

The government objective is to minimize present and expected future values of total government cost, GC, which is a function of fiscal cost and price variability. GC is consequently a broadly defined cost function, including both financial and political or welfare costs:

$$GC_t = g_3(FC_t, PV_t). \tag{13}$$

Thus there are three variables that, in any one year, are outside the control of the government: world price, WP_t, production, Q_t, and opening government stocks, GS_t. In the language of control theory, these are the three state variables that determine the state of the world. Given the state variables, the government chooses the values of three variables that it controls—net procurement, NP_t, imports, M_t, and exports, X_t—in order to minimize present and expected future values of total government cost, GC_t. Future values are discounted. The latter three variables are termed "control variables" in the control-theory literature.

Together, the state variables and the control variables determine the remaining variables. This system is optimized by stochastic dynamic programming. Inequality constraints on imports, exports, and government stocks make certainty equivalent methods, such as those used by Arzac and Wilkinson (1980), inappropriate.

The individual functions are as follows. Production, Q_t, is an exogenous, stochastic, normally distributed random variable. Thus, the costs of government policy are modeled for good, bad, and normal production years. For simplicity, neither supply nor demand is assumed to shift regularly over time. This assumption is useful if the expected growth rates of supply and demand are reasonably close to each other, leading to a normal-production-year equilibrium price that moves only slowly. Such is the case for Pakistan in the short run, as shown above. Because of this assumption, the cost figures are slightly understated, and the volumes mentioned for imports and stocks will grow over time. The assumption is necessary in order to allow the dynamic programming algorithm to stabilize over time. Adjustment of the stock volumes for expected future production growth is carried out below. The demand curve, equation (9), is assumed to have constant elasticity.

Food aid, which covers a set proportion of the shortfall in domestic supply in bad years, is received by the government and is one part of government imports. Sensitivity of the results to the presence or absence of food aid is tested below.

Fiscal costs are calculated as follows. The government's net procurement is multiplied by the price at which the grain is bought or sold. Thus, any costs incurred by the government in both buying and selling in the same market year are not included, since this is an interannual model. Net costs of foreign trade—both exports and imports—are calculated in a similar manner, adjusting for the difference between import and export parity. Foreign exchange is valued at a set premium for both imports and exports. Storage fees are a constant amount per ton of interannual storage. In addition, at the conclusion of the final year of each 10-year cycle in the simulation, a cost is incurred for rebuilding the stock to its opening level in year 1 of the simulation in order to facilitate comparison of different policies.

World price is modeled as a random walk, with movements independent of domestic production. It is particularly important that next year's expected price is close to this year's actual price; otherwise, the optimizing model will engage in speculative behavior.

Price variability, equation (12), is defined as the square root of the average squared deviation of actual price from the target price. This equals the standard deviation of price if the target price equals the ex post mean price. This is the simplest model that has two desirable characteristics: symmetry and increasing penalties for larger deviations. Symmetry is important, since the government is sensitive to the needs of both farmers and consumers. Increasing penalties are appropriate, since a very large change in price is considerably more undesirable than multiple smaller price changes. People starve and governments fall when prices rise dramatically, not when prices move marginally.

Government cost as defined in equation (13) is taken to be a weighted sum of fiscal cost and price variability, with the weight on price variability so that the monetary unit becomes the numeraire of the system. The weight is unknown, representing the relative preference of the government for saving money versus stabilizing prices. Different values of the weight are tested, each representing a different set of government priorities, with the results clarifying how the optimal policy adjusts to different political preferences. This allows for the measurement of the trade-off between the two government objectives.

During the optimization procedure, the algorithm finds the values of government procurement, offtake, and foreign trade that minimize the cost function for every modeled combination of domestic production, world price, and opening stocks. The dynamic programming procedure continues until the optimal policy for one year is the same as the optimal policy for the next year. Thus the outcome of the optimization procedure is a policy that does not vary from year to year. This policy is discrete, however, since the procedure only considers selected possible values for production, world price, and the other variables. Consequently, the discrete policy is interpolated linearly, so as to be continuous, and simulated over 300 10-year cycles of random production and world price. The values of the objectives are calculated in the simulation, and results are reported in the tables and the graphs.

For the values of specific parameters, see Appendix 1, Table 29.

Optimal Policies versus Price Band Policies

Most government price stabilization schemes have tried to stabilize prices within a band. That is, a maximum price and minimum price are set, with the government promising to enter the market with sufficient purchases or sales to keep the domestic price from moving outside those limits. Normally, no government intervention is assumed if the price stays between the maximum and minimum. On the foreign trade side, it is frequently proposed that imports should be triggered by a minimum stock size and exports triggered when some maximum stock size is reached.

To show how the optimal policies differ from these simple price band/buffer stock policies, one of the 300 10-year cycles of the simulation for both types of policies is presented in Table 12. Both policies target a price of Rs85 per 40 kilograms, and over all 300 cycles their average levels of price variability are equal. The price band/buffer stock policy has stock triggers for imports and exports at 0 and 200,000 tons, respectively. The optimal policy costs about Rs85 million less annually over all 300 cycles than this price band policy.

For this particular cycle, the optimal policy costs about Rs60 million less annually. Three years out of 10, however, the price band policy is substantially cheaper than the optimal policy. In each of the 3 years—years 2, 6, and 10—the optimal policy opens a bad production year with no stocks, while the price band policy has substantial stocks. These years cannot be looked at in isolation. The only reason that the price band policy is able to outperform the optimal policy in year 10, for example, is because it failed to earn money from exports in year 9. The problem is dynamic, and the policies can only be judged in a dynamic context. The distribution of prices is dramatically different in the two policies. In 7 out of 10 years, the price band policy is at either its

Table 12—Simulation of optimal and price band policies: one cycle

Year	World Price (US$/ metric ton)	Production (1,000 metric tons)	Net Procurement (1,000 metric tons)		Domestic Price (Rs/40 kilograms)		Net Imports (Including Aid) (1,000 metric tons)		Closing Stocks		Annual Cost (Rs million)		Present Value of Sum of Annual Costs (Rs million)	
			(1)	(2)	(1)	(2)	(1)	(2)	(1)	(2)	(1)	(2)	(1)	(2)
0	...	...	...	...	...	...	...	...	100	100	...	...	...	...
1	102	12,869	-117	0	85	88	17	0	0	100	-205	43	-205	43
2	92	11,353	-1,360	-1,349	92	92	1,359	1,249	0	0	-773	-1,027	-927	-917
3	68	13,681	230	376	76	79	-117	-176	113	200	380	669	-595	-333
4	68	13,891	376	586	75	79	-285	-586	204	200	538	723	-156	258
5	84	13,308	-23	3	78	79	-180	-3	0	200	-257	87	-352	324
6	85	11,284	-1,450	-1,418	91	92	1,450	1,218	0	0	-904	-1,396	-997	-671
7	108	12,991	-3	0	85	85	3	0	0	0	2	0	-995	-671
8	135	13,136	144	0	85	82	-144	0	0	0	1	0	-995	-671
9	157	13,474	517	169	86	79	-517	0	0	169	-199	404	-1,110	-436
10	151	12,605	-69	-97	93	92	69	0	0	72	85	-192	-1,064	-541
Replace stock adjustment	...	...	...	...	...	...	...	...	...	...	187	52	-962	-512
Average annual cost	...	...	...	...	...	...	...	...	...	...	-128	-68	...	...

Source: Author's calculations.

Note: (1) = optimal policy; (2) = price band policy.

maximum or minimum price. The optimal policy, on the other hand, has 4 years when the price is within one rupee of the target price. In 3 years, the price resulting from the optimal policy is below the minimum price of the price band policy. In each case, supplies are abundant and the world price is low. Similarly, the one year when the optimal policy price is above the price band's maximum is when production is low and the world price is high.

Year 9 is perhaps the best example of why the optimal policy is more efficient than the price band policy. Production is fairly high—high enough so that the price band minimum is reached and that policy withdraws 169,000 tons from the market, placing all of it into storage. In contrast, the optimal policy has a net procurement of 517,000 tons, bringing the domestic price very close to the target price, and exports the entire amount at a profit, since the world price is US$157 per ton. The net result is earnings of Rs200 million for the optimal policy and losses of Rs400 million for the price band policy, with the price outcome also preferable under the optimal policy.

These examples suggest that *the optimal policy is superior because of greater responsiveness to the world price and domestic production.* This suggestion is explored in more detail below, after a consideration of average results for all of the cycles.

Optimization Results

Table 13 presents results of the optimization model for the base case, in which production instability is 6 percent and food aid is available. The first two columns of the table present the government objectives of price variability and fiscal cost. The third and fourth columns present two other items of concern to the government that

Table 13—Optimal policy results: base case

| | | | | | | Components of Cost | | |
Price Variability	Average Annual Fiscal Cost	Standard Deviation of Cost	Average Imports, 10-Year Period	Average Closing Stock	Storage Costs	Domestic Costs of Foreign Trade	Net Other Domestic Costs	Direct Foreign Exchange Losses
(Rs/40 kilograms)	(Rs million)		(million metric tons)	(1,000 metric tons)		(Rs million)		(US$ million)
14.7[a]	−164.5[ab]	138[a]	1.76[a]	0[a]	0.0[a]	193[a]	212.5[a]	−30.5[a]
5.9	−44.9	125	1.95	34	7.4	171	−14.5	−11.2
5.4	−26.5	128	2.03	30	6.6	179	−7.7	−10.9
4.8	−4.5	132	2.11	37	7.8	186	−4.3	−10.4
4.2	19.9	137	2.20	40	8.3	194	2.6	−9.9
3.7	43.6	140	2.27	43	8.8	201	12.1	−9.5
3.1	70.9	144	2.39	23	5.1	214	22.5	−9.1
2.6	94.0	148	2.48	24	5.1	220	25.2	−8.4
1.9	123.6	155	2.57	26	5.4	229	35.4	−7.8
1.4	150.1	163	2.66	26	5.5	236	44.4	−7.3
0.9	174.7	167	2.77	12	2.2	246	49.4	−6.6

Source: Author's calculations.
Notes: In the base case, food aid is included and production variability is 6 percent. The 1985 exchange rate was about Rs16.00 = US$1.00.
[a] Free-market result.
[b] This amount is not fiscal cost but net cost to the economy of domestic and foreign wheat marketing.

are not included in the objective function: the variability of fiscal cost and average total imports during 10 years.[19] The fifth column presents average closing stocks.

The last four columns of Table 13 present a breakdown of fiscal costs into four components. The first component, storage costs, consists of the direct cost of storing wheat, including the value of physical losses and the costs of putting the grain into and taking it out of the storage facility. The second component, the domestic costs of foreign trade, includes charges for transportation, bagging, and handling of wheat exports, and the excess costs of handling wheat imports beyond the costs of handling domestic wheat. The third component, net other domestic costs, is composed primarily of the difference between the value of domestic sales and the value of domestic purchases. The implicit value of the stock change between the first and tenth years is also included in this component. The last column gives the direct foreign exchange losses, expressed in U.S. dollars. A negative value indicates a gain in foreign exchange on average through wheat operations. This component includes the cost of foreign shipping on all imports (including food aid).

The first row of Table 13 presents results of a run that attempts to describe the free-market solution. As shown in Gustafson (1958, 48-49), maximization of a producer/consumer surplus function yields the free-market solution. This technique has been used here. There is no government intervention in either domestic or foreign trade, necessitating the change in objective function. This run can be considered a test of the stability of domestic prices under a free-trade regime.

The results indicate that the government has stabilized prices compared with what would have been the case in the absence of intervention. Price variability in the nonintervention case is almost Rs15 per 40 kilograms; this implies that, if the average harvest-time price were Rs80 per 40 kilograms, one year out of six the price would be greater than Rs95 and one year out of six the price would be less than Rs65. Column 2 for this row is not fiscal cost but net cost to the economy of domestic and foreign wheat marketing. A large profit is made, most of it in foreign exchange, as shown in the last column. On average, the nonintervention solution raises the average domestic price above its equilibrium level by buying more than it sells domestically and exporting the difference in years of high world prices.

The substantial change in average price possible in the nonintervention case calls into question the model's assumption about no supply response to price. Adding a supply response would cause profits made under this scenario to increase further, as more would be grown—and thus exported—in periods of high world prices. It would also increase average imports, as domestic production would decrease in low-world-price periods, which are the only times when imports take place in the nonintervention scenario. Price variability should be unaffected by such a change.[20]

The other 10 rows in Table 13 present optimal solutions under different possible relative preferences between price stability and low fiscal expenditure. There are several general observations to be made about the results.

---

[19] Column 3 presents the standard deviation of the average price over 10 years, not the standard deviation of the annual cost. The latter figure can be approximated by multiplying the number in column 3 by the square root of 10 (about 3.2).

[20] For all optimization runs except the nonintervention case, ignoring supply response is reasonable because of the resulting simplicity of the model and the absence of significant changes in expected price from year to year (Pinckney 1988b).

First, *fiscal costs increase substantially as price variability is limited.* This is the trade-off between the two government objectives included in the model. On average for the range considered here, the trade-off is about Rs45 million annually for each one-rupee decrease in price variability. The trade-off increases slightly as price variability declines. Consequently, a policy that would efficiently keep harvest-time prices between Rs70.00 and Rs90.00 per 40 kilograms for 9 years out of 10 costs about Rs220 million more per year than a policy that keeps those prices between Rs78.50 and Rs81.50.[21]

Second, *government can stabilize prices significantly at no cost on average.* When price variability is about 4.6—that is, harvest-time prices are kept between Rs72.50 and Rs87.50 per 40 kilograms for 9 out of 10 years—average costs are zero. The government on average earns foreign exchange and spends domestic currency.

Third, *the variability of cost is quite high.* Over a 10-year period, the expected average annual cost of the policy with price variability of 0.9 is about Rs175 million, but since the standard deviation of this cost is Rs167 million, there is a one-in-six chance that the cost would average less than Rs8 million annually, and a one-in-six chance that the cost would average more than Rs332 million annually. In any single year, there is a one-in-six chance that the cost will be greater than Rs700 million, and a similar chance that the policy will make a profit of more than Rs350 million.[22] The variability of cost increases somewhat as price variability decreases. Thus, even though the government might aim at a policy with zero cost, over a long period of years the costs could be high.

Fourth, all of the efficient policies have net foreign exchange earnings on the wheat account, but *there is a negative relationship between price stability and foreign exchange earnings.* The extent to which this result is dependent on the assumptions about food aid is tested below.

Finally, *average closing stocks are exceptionally low,* ranging from 12,000 to 43,000 tons. As a consequence, storage costs are quite low relative to other costs. Recall that these stocks are only those for interannual supply stabilization; actual stock levels will be higher because of the other reasons for storage. Supply stabilization stocks are held in these policies only when the world price of wheat is less than US$80 per ton. In real terms, such a price would be a record low for wheat.

When the world price is US$60 per ton, the policies with higher price variability hold as much as 400,000 tons of stock before exporting the excess. No policies studied here hold more than 600,000 tons under any circumstances. The reasons for this relatively low level of interannual stockholding are explored in the following section.

Rationale for Interannual Stockholding

The policy-decision variables under the government's control can be considered as sequential. The government opens the marketing year with some opening stock, S_{t-1}. Given production, a certain amount is procured and sold, leaving a net level of procurement, PC_t.[23] The sum $S_{t-1} + PC_t$ is termed here "available supply." If available supply

---

[21] In order to calculate these numbers, the price variability is multiplied by 1.645, since 90 percent of a normal distribution falls within this number of standard deviations of the mean.

[22] The annual cost figures are calculated by taking the standard deviation of the 10-year average cost, Rs167 million, and multiplying it by the square root of 10 to produce the standard deviation of annual cost.

[23] The decision variable is considered in volume terms here for consistency with the trade/stock decision variable. As there is a one-to-one correspondence between price and consumption, however, this decision variable determines price in conjunction with production.

42

is negative, the government must import to meet domestic demand. If available supply is positive, the government can decide how much to export and how much to store.

This decision, then, involves comparing the known value of exporting the commodity this year with the expected value of holding the commodity for possible sale next year. The value of 1 ton of available supply this year is simply the present export parity price, XP_t. The expected value next year is a weighted average of the possible uses of the stock next year. These possibilities are as follows:

1. Export next year. The expected value today for exporting next year is $[E(XP_{t+1}) -$ STCH]/D, where E(.) is the expectations operator, XP is export parity as above, STCH is the cost of storing the commodity for one year, and D is the discount rate applied because of the time value of money.[24] Assuming that the government has no inside information about world wheat prices, it is reasonable to assume that the expected price next year equals the present price; that is, $E(XP_{t+1}) = XP_t$. Thus, this component of the value of the stored commodity can be simplified to $(XP_t - STCH)/D$.

2. Sell domestically next year, displacing imports. In this case, the value of the commodity is import parity next year, as opposed to next year's domestic price. If imports are displaced, the only difference between storing or not storing this year is not having to import next year. Consequently, the value is $[E(MP_{t+1}) - STCH]/D$, which can be simplified as above to $(MP_t - STCH)/D$, with MP being import parity.

3. Store again next year. This can be calculated by setting up possibilities (1) and (2) for several years into the future until the discount rate minimizes the importance of additional years, and then working backward to calculate the value of storing an additional year. These are the only possible uses for the stock.[25] The value of storing, therefore, is the weighted average of these three components, with the probability of each occurring next year used as the weights.[26] The decision will depend on the value of the parameters and the probabilities.

The dynamic programming exercise can be considered a complex method for determining the probabilities of the different reasons for storage. As an example, however, assume that the probability of exporting the stock next year equals the probability of displacing imports next year at 0.45. Thus the probability of storing again next year equals 0.1. Given other parameters (see Appendix 1, Table 29) and a world price of US$110 per ton, the values are as follows:

Use of Stock	Present Value per Ton	Probability
Export next year	Rs1,130	0.45
Displace imports next year	Rs2,181	0.45
Store again next year	Rs1,101	0.10
Weighted average	Rs1,600	. . .
Export this year	Rs1,663	. . .

---

[24] Analytically, based on standard economic theory, it is inappropriate to apply both a discount rate and an interest rate in an interannual model in real prices. See Gardner 1979.

[25] The fourth possibility, sell domestically next year, not displacing imports, is only possible if the government allows the domestic price to be affected by its opening stock level. Such behavior does occur in the optimal policies to a minor extent; it is left out to simplify the discussion.

[26] In the model formulated above, government storage has a negative effect on the amount of food aid received. The expected negative value of this amount should also be included in the calculation, but is excluded for clarity of exposition.

As the world price declines, the difference between the value of exporting and the value of storing decreases. For these probabilities, the two are equal when the world price is US$63 per ton. Thus, if these probabilities were correct, no wheat would be stored with world prices above US$63.

Each additional ton stored, however, has a different set of probabilities for its disposal in the next year. As more is kept in store, the probability of each additional ton displacing imports next year declines, since a higher percentage of production shortfalls will be met with already existing stocks. Similarly, the probabilities of exporting next year and storing again increase. This decreases the incentive to hold additional stock. Small changes in probabilities have a large impact on the world price at which additional grain will be put in store. For example, suppose that the probabilities for the three outcomes above change from 0.45, 0.45, 0.10 for the first ton stored to 0.46, 0.43, 0.11 for the 100th ton stored. In this case, the world price at which storage takes place declines from US$63 to US$48, even though the probability change is small.

Note that the decision of whether or not to store the wheat makes no reference to the price paid domestically to purchase the crop. Unfortunately, for accounting reasons grain marketing authorities in some countries have been restricted from exporting because of the accounting loss they would incur if their stock of grain were exported at a price beneath their purchase price. Valuing the stock at its purchase price is an accounting fiction, however. Economically, the value of the stock is its most profitable possible use, and this value has been determined in the calculation above. Thus, it saves money at times to export rather than store, even though an accountant may have to enter a loss in the marketing board's books.

Sensitivity of Optimal Stock Size to Assumptions

Assumptions about food aid and the variability of production will affect the average stock size that results from the optimal policies. This section tests to see what effect ignoring food aid and assuming a higher variability of production have on storage and other outcomes.

As shown in the first section of this chapter, assuming a coefficient of variation for production of 6 percent is reasonable. There is some indication, however, that variability has been increasing over time. For future planning, testing the sensitivity of storage size to production variability of 7 percent is desirable.

In terms of the analysis in the previous section, a rise in production variability will increase both the probability of exporting the stock next year and the probability of using the stock to displace imports. Although these two effects are offsetting to some extent, an equal increase in both probabilities raises the world price at which storage is profitable. For example, in the table on p. 43, if these two probabilities are both raised from 0.45 to 0.48, the world price at which storage becomes profitable increases from US$63 to US$87.

Table 14 presents optimization results with all parameters the same as in Table 13, but with production variability increased to 7 percent. Figure 3 shows these results graphically, along with the results for no food aid.

The production variability change increases stockholding only slightly. Costs are almost identical at the higher range of price variability, although cost differences increase to about Rs15 million annually at lower levels of price variability (this is clearer in Figure 3 than in Table 14 because of differences in price variability). These cost differences are small, partly because the higher production variability induces increased food aid. The higher variability raises average imports and exports by almost 20 percent,

Table 14—Optimal policy results: production instability at 7 percent

Price Variability	Average Annual Fiscal Cost	Standard Deviation of Cost	Average Imports, 10-Year Period	Average Closing Stock	Storage Costs	Domestic Costs of Foreign Trade	Net Other Domestic Costs	Direct Foreign Exchange Losses
						Components of Cost		
(Rs/40 kilograms)	(Rs million)		(million metric tons)	(1,000 metric tons)		(Rs million)		(US$ million)
6.2	−59.0	150	2.36	40	8.7	205	−30.7	−12.9
5.7	−38.2	154	2.44	35	7.5	214	−21.5	−12.7
5.1	−13.3	158	2.53	41	8.6	221	−15.1	−12.2
4.5	14.5	164	2.63	43	9.1	228	−5.2	−11.6
3.8	42.0	169	2.72	46	9.5	239	5.3	−11.3
3.3	71.3	173	2.85	24	5.2	253	19.0	−11.0
2.7	96.9	177	2.95	25	5.3	260	22.5	−10.2
2.0	130.5	185	3.05	27	5.5	269	35.9	−9.6
1.5	159.7	194	3.14	27	5.6	277	46.9	−9.1
1.0	186.2	197	3.26	13	2.3	288	53.5	−8.4

Source: Author's calculations.

Figure 3—Optimal policy trade-off curves: three variations of parameters

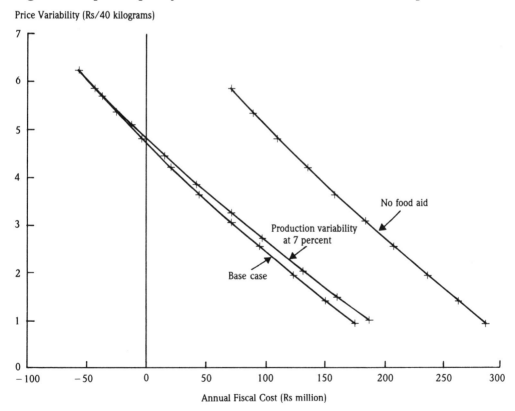

Price Variability (Rs/40 kilograms)

No food aid

Production variability at 7 percent

Base case

Annual Fiscal Cost (Rs million)

45

but this additional foreign trade is conducted with only small losses. Thus, changing the assumption about production variability has little effect on storage or expected fiscal costs.

Assuming no food aid, on the other hand, increases costs substantially and increases average stockholding to about 80,000 tons. In the base case, food aid amounts to about 560,000 tons over a 10-year period, thus constituting about one-fourth of total imports. The removal of this grant adds about Rs110 million to the average annual cost, as displayed in Figure 3. Table 15 shows that the foreign exchange account suffers most in comparison to the base case, as would be expected.

Table 15 shows only average stockholding. For an analysis of storage capacity, maximum stockholding is an important variable. The largest amount stored increases 200,000 tons over the base case, rising to 600,000 tons when the world price is US$60 per ton; as much as 50,000 tons are held when the world price is US$100 per ton. Nevertheless, when the world price is US$110 per ton or higher, no interannual supply stabilization stocks are held, regardless of whether or not food aid is available.

The assumption of no food aid is extreme. For the foreseeable future, Pakistan will be able to arrange for significant amounts of food aid from the international community in poor crop years. The absence of large supply stabilization stocks even in this extreme case strongly indicates that the requirement for this component of stockholding is quite small.

Computing the Value of Additional Storage Space

Despite low average stockholdings, all three sets of optimization results occasionally hold stocks of 400,000-600,000 tons. In the model, neither construction nor depreciation costs are included, since storage space of that amount is assumed to be available already. But in planning for future storage capacity, the question arises, Should Pakistan build 400,000-600,000 tons of storage capacity for supply stabilization besides storage requirements for other uses?

In order to assess the cost advantages of having the additional storage, the optimization model is run with maximum storage capacity constrained. Then the average cost

Table 15—Optimal policy results: no food aid

| | | | | | | Components of Cost | | |
Price Variability	Average Annual Fiscal Cost	Standard Deviation of Cost	Average Imports, 10-Year Period	Average Closing Stock	Storage Costs	Domestic Costs of Foreign Trade	Net Other Domestic Costs	Direct Foreign Exchange Losses
(Rs/40 kilograms)	(Rs million)		(million metric tons)	(1,000 metric tons)		(Rs million)		(US$ million)
5.9	69.7	118	1.87	57	17.5	161	−23.8	−4.6
5.4	88.9	123	1.94	62	17.9	169	−15.5	−4.4
4.8	109.3	130	2.01	69	19.4	174	−14.3	−3.7
4.2	135.2	137	2.09	76	21.2	182	−4.5	−3.4
3.7	157.9	144	2.16	81	22.2	188	2.7	−3.0
3.1	183.0	151	2.25	84	23.2	196	7.8	−2.3
2.6	207.8	158	2.35	82	21.4	205	14.9	−1.8
1.9	237.3	167	2.44	80	21.4	214	25.9	−1.3
1.4	263.2	178	2.51	85	23.5	220	33.4	−0.7
1.0	287.4	184	2.61	80	22.7	227	37.2	0.0

Source: Author's calculations.

of the constrained policy can be compared with the average cost of the unconstrained policy, keeping price variability the same in the two cases. The value of the additional capacity is assessed by comparing the change in fiscal cost.

When this is done, the value of the extra storage space turns out to be small, primarily because of the low percentage of years in which it is used. The average gross benefit ranges from Rs100,000-500,000 annually for each additional 100,000 tons of storage, with the actual number sensitive to the chosen degree of price variability and how much storage has already been built. The Experience, Zor, and Ferguson (1986) study estimates that construction costs are about Rs70 million per 100,000 tons capacity, and maintenance costs are between Rs250,000 and Rs1 million annually. Thus the value to the country of building extra capacity for supply stabilization is barely equal to the maintenance costs of the facility; the benefits do not begin to pay the country back for the capital costs of construction.

Therefore, in terms of planning for future storage requirements, no additional capacity should be built for interannual supply stabilization. If capacity is available, in years of abundant supply and very low world prices it will make sense to store up to a few hundred thousand tons, but the value of always having that capacity available is only equal to average maintenance costs.

Lessons for an Efficient Supply Stabilization Strategy

Characterizing the Efficient Policies

A policy produced by the optimization process meets the government objectives of price stability and low fiscal cost better than any alternative policy, given a set of government preferences. These policies, however, are difficult to understand and describe. Simpler policies are required if the optimization exercise is to have an effect on the policymaking process. A detailed examination of what makes the optimal policies efficient can provide clues for the design of simpler, yet efficient, policies.

Recall that government intervention can be considered as two separate steps: first, making a decision about net procurement, and second, allocating available supply between exports and carryover stocks. The efficient rule for supply allocation is already clear. When aid is included in the model, the optimal policies do not hold any stock when world prices are US$80 per ton or above. Thus the decision on how to allocate available supply between stocks and exports is simple for most world prices: hold no stocks.

The earlier decision—determining net procurement and the domestic price—is more difficult to characterize. The simulation of one 10-year cycle in Table 12 suggests that a key difference between an optimal policy and a price band policy is the degree to which the domestic price responds to the world price and to domestic production. For example, the price band policy reaches its minimum price in years 3, 4, 5, and 9, when domestic production is high. The optimal policy also produces low prices in the first three cases, when world prices are low, but offers farmers a much higher price in year 9, when profitable exports are possible.

In order to examine this relationship further, optimal net procurement is plotted against production for one of the optimal policies, holding world price within a fairly narrow range (Figure 4).[27] The figure suggests that the relationship between these two

---

[27] Since only nine possible production levels are modeled in the optimization process, these points are all taken from the simulation of the interpolated optimal policy.

Figure 4—Net procurement function

Net Procurement (million metric tons)

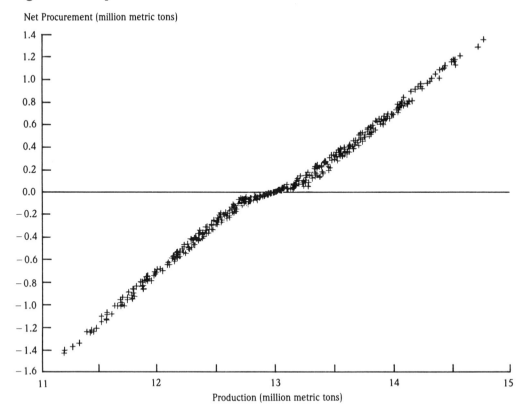

Production (million metric tons)

Note: Price variability is 5.9. The figure includes all observations in the simulation in which the world price is between US$100 and US$120.

variables is close to linear, but that a kinked linear relationship with a flatter section close to mean production may model the optimal relationship more closely. This hypothesis is investigated using regression analysis in Table 16. The regression results should clarify the key elements in the superiority of the optimal policies over the price band policies.

In this table, five regression equations are reported for each of three levels of price variability. The dependent variable in each case is net procurement in years of the simulation of the interpolated optimal policy. As there are 300 10-year cycles, there are 3,000 possible observations. In order for the regression results to reflect accurately the optimal policy, however, it is necessary to exclude observations that may bias results. First, years with values for world price or production that are far from those modeled in the optimization process are excluded. Since the optimization process considers only world prices between US$60 and US$180 and production between 11.2 and 14.8 million tons, only observations in which the world price is between US$50 and US$190 and production is between 11.1 and 14.9 million tons are included. These restrictions lower the total number of observations to 2,587.

The second restriction on observations has to do with opening stocks. In this case, there is no problem with the range of the stock variable but with the distribution of

Table 16—Net procurement function

Level of Production	Constant	World Price	Production (Qt)	R²	Standard Error of Regression	N
(1,000 metric tons)			Regression Results for Price Variability at 0.9			
(1) All production levels	−46.42	0.60 (0.44)	. . .	0.001	708.7	2,287
(2) All production levels	−12,496	0.62 (0.01)	0.956 (0.0003)	1.000	12.3	2,287
(3) (a) Qt > 13,300	−12,813	0.69 (0.01)	0.978 (0.001)	0.999	9.3	821
(b) 12,700 < Qt < 13,300	−11,969	0.50 (0.01)	0.917 (0.002)	0.996	10.2	692
(c) Qt < 12,700	−12,729	0.66 (0.01)	0.976 (0.001)	0.999	8.5	774
			Regression Results for Price Variability at 3.1			
(1) All production levels	−205.3	2.06 (0.40)	. . .	0.012	632.0	2,287
(2) All production levels	−11,300	2.07 (0.02)	0.852 (0.001)	0.997	34.2	2,287
(3) (a) Qt > 13,300	−12,368	2.59 (0.01)	0.925 (0.001)	0.999	12.5	821
(b) 12,700 < Qt < 13,300	−9,350	1.54 (0.02)	0.707 (0.004)	0.979	19.1	692
(c) Qt < 12,700	−12,274	2.06 (0.01)	0.933 (0.001)	0.999	9.0	774
			Regression Results for Price Variability at 5.9			
(1) All production levels	−415.5	3.91 (0.33)	. . .	0.057	531.5	2,287
(2) All production levels	−9,686	3.92 (0.04)	0.712 (0.002)	0.986	64.2	2,287
(3) (a) Qt > 13,300	−11,433	5.13 (0.02)	0.827 (0.002)	0.995	23.2	821
(b) 12,700 < Qt < 13,300	−6,419	2.78 (0.04)	0.471 (0.008)	0.914	37.2	692
(c) Qt < 12,700	−11,529	3.73 (0.02)	0.866 (0.002)	0.997	19.3	774

Source: Author's calculations.
Notes: The figures in parentheses are the standard errors of the estimated coefficients. Regressions are for (1) world price alone on entire sample, (2) world price and production on entire sample, and (3) world price and production on three subsets of the sample.

the size of stocks in the observations. Opening stocks in year 1 of each cycle are 100,000 tons, while average closing stocks are much lower. Thus, one-tenth of the observations have stocks of 100. In order to avoid a bias due to a large number of relatively high stock years, only the last nine years of each simulation are included in the regression, lowering the total number of observations to 2,287.

Regressions are reported for world price alone on the entire sample, for world price and production on the entire sample, and for world price and production on three subsets of the sample: production less than 12.7 million tons, greater than 13.3 million tons, and between those two values. This final partitioning is consistent with the pattern seen in Figure 4.[28]

The regressions help to explain how the optimal policies act and how such policies change as the government preference for price stability changes. Net procurement is more responsive to the world price and less responsive to production when price variability is high. Estimating three regressions—one each for low, medium, and high production—improves the fit substantially,[29] and produces coefficients for each production level that are significantly different from corresponding coefficients at different production levels. In each case, the response of net procurement to a change in the world price or production is less in the middle of the production range than it is at either extreme. The change in the coefficients becomes more dramatic as price variability increases.

The primary rationale for the decreased sensitivity to production and world price when production is close to normal is that the government would prefer several small price changes rather than a single, sharp rise in price. A policy that allows a sudden 50 percent change in price once in five years while holding prices constant in the other four is much worse than a policy that allows a 10 percent change in price in each of five years. Thus, the government preference for price stability is assumed to penalize deviations from the target price at an increasing rate (proportional to the square of the deviation). Consequently, the optimal policies do not force consumption to change as much when the price is close to the target as when the price is further from the target. An efficient government policy would do the same.

The implied degree of price sensitivity to world price and domestic production can be calculated. As stated in the methodology section above, for any given level of production, consumption is determined by net procurement. Thus, changes in production and world price affect consumption by the negative of their coefficients in the net procurement equations. Consequently, a coefficient of world price of 0.62 (Table 16, equation [2], price variability at 0.9) requires that consumption decrease by 6,200 tons if the world price increases by US$10 per ton. Assuming a base of 13 million tons for total consumption, this is a $-6/13,000 = -0.046$ percent change. Dividing this percentage by the price elasticity of -0.3 yields a required price increase of 0.15 percent, or Rs0.13 assuming a prior price of Rs85 per 40 kilograms. A similar calculation shows that the highest sensitivity of domestic price to world price, which occurs when price variability equals 5.9 and production is greater than 13.3 million tons, implies a price change of Rs1.12 per 40 kilograms when the world price goes up by US$10 per ton.

On the production side, a coefficient of production of 0.978—the highest in Table 16—implies that 97,800 tons out of a 100,000-ton increase in production would be procured. Consequently, consumption would rise by only 2,200 tons. Continuing as above, this implies a 0.017 percentage change in consumption and a -0.056 percentage change in price, or about Rs-0.05 per 40 kilograms. Similarly, the lowest coefficient of production in the table—0.471—implies a change of Rs-1.15 per 40 kilograms for the same 100,000-ton increase in production.

---

[28] Pinckney 1988b presents results for Kenya that include sensitivity of net procurement to opening stocks. Similar regressions were run for Pakistan, but stock levels are so low that the contribution of the variable is negligible.

[29] The goodness of fit should be judged here by comparing regression standard errors rather than R^2's, since the range of the dependent variable changes in the partitioned regression.

Thus the optimal policies can be characterized quite well. The optimal domestic intervention of the government can be approximated by three linear relationships linking net procurement to production and the world price. The available supply that results from adding this net procurement to opening stocks should be exported unless world prices reach new record lows. The next section discusses how this characterization can aid in policy design.

Designing a Simple and Efficient Policy

It is not reasonable to propose that a government adopt the policies that result from an optimization routine. Such policies are difficult to describe and complicated to implement. The government has an objective of "simplicity of policy" that is difficult, if not impossible, to build into the objective function of an optimization procedure. Consequently, there is a trade-off between the complexity of a policy and its efficiency. There is a need to examine the elements that make the optimal policies more efficient, and to measure the degree to which each element contributes to decreasing fiscal cost while holding price variability constant. In this way, decisionmakers can decide whether or not the complexity introduced by an additional element is worth the associated savings in cost.

The regression results and the knowledge about the relative importance of stocks and exports suggest that there are five elements that make the optimal policies more efficient than the simplistic price band/buffer stock policies discussed above: stockholdings should be quite low; the maximum stock level should be sensitive to the world price, and decline to 0 at some world price; the domestic price should be sensitive to the world price; the domestic price should be sensitive to domestic production; and the degree of sensitivity to world price and production should depend on whether production is high, average, or low.

These elements are listed in order of increasing difficulty of implementation. The first two do not affect the domestic price and are thus invisible to most persons in the country.

Table 17 presents the results of adding these elements one by one to a simple price band/buffer stock policy. Figure 5 presents the same information in graphic form for the three levels of price variability, while Figure 6 details the results for the middle case. In the figures, the optimal policies (that is, policy 7) are connected by a line, and the other numbers correspond to the policy numbers in Table 17. When policies 2 and 5 do not appear in Figures 5 and 6, their costs are virtually equal to the costs of policies 3 and 4.

The improvements are much more dramatic for the relatively high price-variability case than for the low price-variability case. As prices become more stable, the scope for policy modifications becomes less. All policies with a price variability of zero would have a coefficient of 1.0 in the net procurement function; that is, all changes in production would be absorbed by changes in procurement in order to hold the price constant. Thus, the net procurement function for a simple price band/buffer stock policy begins to approach the same shape as the optimal policy when price variability approaches zero. Consequently, when price variability is 0.9, the gain in moving from a price band policy that never holds stocks (policy 2) to a policy in which net procurement is sensitive to both production and the world price at levels dependent on production (policy 6) is only Rs13 million annually. In contrast, when price variability is 5.9, the difference between these two types of policies is Rs63 million.

At all levels of price variability, lowering the maximum stock level in the price band/buffer stock scheme from 150,000 tons to zero saves large amounts, ranging

Table 17—Components of an efficient policy

Policy		Annual Cost	Improvement	Foreign Exchange Earnings
		(Rs million)		(US$ million)
(a) Price variability Rs 0.9 per 40 kilograms				
Policy 1 (a):	Simple price band with 150,000 metric tons buffer stock	207	. . .	4.0
Policy 2 (a):	Policy 1 with no buffer stock	186	22	5.6
Policy 3 (a):	Policy 1 with variable buffer stock, size dependent on world price	185	1	5.6
Policy 4 (a):	Policy 3 with price band adjusting to world price	178	7	8.8
Policy 5 (a):	Policy 4 adding sensitivity to domestic production	174	3	6.6
Policy 6 (a):	Policy 5 with degree of sensitivity to world price and production depending on production	173	1	6.7
Policy 7 (a):	Optimal policy	175	−2	6.6
(b) Price variability Rs 3.1 per 40 kilograms				
Policy 1 (b):	Simple price band with 150,000 metric tons buffer stock	134	. . .	4.4
Policy 2 (b):	Policy 1 with no buffer stock	108	26	6.0
Policy 3 (b):	Policy 1 with variable buffer stock, size dependent on world price	107	1	3.5
Policy 4 (b):	Policy 3 with price band adjusting to world price	75	32	10.9
Policy 5 (b):	Policy 4 adding sensitivity to domestic production	75	0	9.3
Policy 6 (b):	Policy 5 with degree of sensitivity to world price and production depending on production	71	4	9.4
Policy 7 (b):	Optimal policy	71	0	9.1
(c) Price variability Rs 5.9 per 40 kilograms				
Policy 1 (c):	Simple price band with 150,000 metric tons buffer stock	54	. . .	4.6
Policy 2 (c):	Policy 1 with no buffer stock	21	32	6.3
Policy 3 (c):	Policy 1 with variable buffer stock, size dependent on world price	21	0	6.3
Policy 4 (c):	Policy 3 with price band adjusting to world price	−34	55	11.8
Policy 5 (c):	Policy 4 adding sensitivity to domestic production	−32	−2	11.8
Policy 6 (c):	Policy 5 with degree of sensitivity to world price and production depending on production	−42	9	11.9
Policy 7 (c):	Optimal policy	−45	3	11.2

(continued)

Table 17—Continued

Notes: Policies 1(a), 2(a), and 3(a) have a price band of 1.12 percent. Policies 1(b), 2(b), and 3(b) have a price band of 3.82 percent. Policies 1(c), 2(c), and 3(c) have a price band of 7.72 percent.

Policies 3(a), 3(b), and 3(c) have a buffer stock of zero when the world price is above US$80 per metric ton. The maximum buffer stock for policies 3(a), 3(b), and 3(c) rises to 150,000 metric tons as the world price drops to US$30 per metric ton.

The price band for policy 4(a) is 0.78 percent. The domestic price is adjusted 13 paisa per 40 kilograms for every US$10 change in the world price. The price band for policy 4(b) is 3.12 percent. The domestic price is adjusted 45 paisa per 40 kilograms for every US$10 change in the world price. The price band for policy 4(c) is 6.82 percent. The domestic price is adjusted 85 paisa per 40 kilograms for every US$10 change in the world price.

In policy 5(a) the domestic price moves 13 paisa per 40 kilograms for each US$10 change in the world price, and 9 paisa per 40 kilograms for each 100,000-metric-ton increase in production. In policy 5(b) the domestic price moves 45 paisa per 40 kilograms for each US$10 change in the world price, and 32 paisa per 40 kilograms for each 100,000-metric-ton increase in production. In policy 5(c) the domestic price moves 85 paisa per 40 kilograms for each US$10 change in the world price, and 63 paisa per 40 kilograms for each 100,000-metric-ton increase in production.

In policies 6(a), 6(b), and 6(c) the domestic price moves with respect to the world price and domestic production in accord with regressions (3)(a), (3)(b), and (3)(c) of Table 16.

Parts may not add to totals because of rounding.

Figure 5—Efficient policy adjustments for three levels of price variability

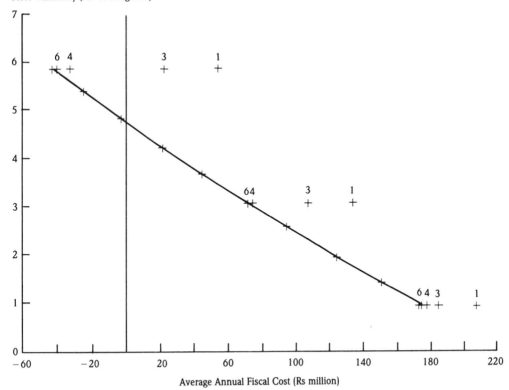

Notes: Policy 1 is the price band policy with a buffer stock of 150,000 metric tons. Policy 3 is the price band policy with a variable-sized buffer stock whose size is dependent on the world price. Policy 4 is policy 3 with a price band that moves with changes in the world price. Policy 6 is policy 4 with the price band sensitive to production and world price, but with the degree of sensitivity dependent on the level of production.

Figure 6—Efficient policy adjustments for middle level of price variability

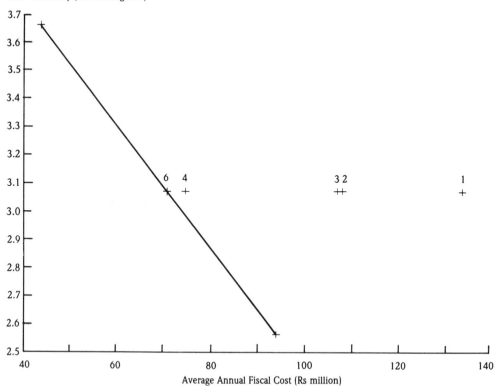

Notes: Policy 1 is the price band policy with a buffer stock of 150,000 metric tons. Policy 2 is the price band policy with no buffer stock. Policy 3 is the price band policy with a variable-sized buffer stock whose size is dependent on the world price. Policy 4 is policy 3 with a price band that moves with changes in the world price. Policy 6 is policy 4 with the price band sensitive to production and world price, but with the degree of sensitivity dependent on the level of production.

from Rs22 million to Rs32 million annually. Changing the policy by allowing some stocks to be held when the world price is low (policy 3) has virtually no effect on the cost, since years with the world price below US$80 per ton are few.

Allowing the domestic price to respond to the world price (policy 4) has the greatest effect of any single policy change for the higher levels of price variability. This policy adjustment also exhibits the largest variation in effect, as shown in Figure 5. The improvement from policy 3 to policy 4 is only Rs7 million annually when price variability is 0.9; the improvement is Rs32 million and Rs55 million annually when price variability is 3.1 and 5.9, respectively. This disparity is explained by the large difference in sensitivity to the world price among the different optimal policies. When price variability is 5.9, domestic consumption responds more than six times as much to a change in the world price as when price variability is only 0.9. The policy change is more dramatic and consequently more effective at higher levels of price variability.

Adding sensitivity to domestic production—moving from policy 4 to policy 5—has only a small effect and actually produces an inferior policy when price variability is 5.9. In interpreting this result, it is important to understand the differences between policy 4 and policy 5. Policy 4 consists of a domestic price band that moves up and down depending on the world price. Holding world price constant, the net procurement function looks like the one shown in Figure 7. If the price is to be held between P_{max} and P_{min}, the net procurement function has a slope of one when production is less than Q_{low}, a slope of zero when production is between Q_{low} and Q_{high}, and a slope of one again when production is above Q_{high}. On the other hand, policy 5 basically implements the net purchases function estimated in equations (2) of Table 16, which is a straight line when world price is constant. Given the pattern for the optimal net purchases function shown in Figure 4, it is clear that the function implied by the price band policy is closer to optimal than the straight line of policy 5. As price variability declines, however, the middle section of the optimal policy's net procurement curve becomes less flat, and a straight line eventually becomes a better approximation than the zero-sloped segment of a price band policy.

The policy that is sensitive to the world price alone—policy 4—is thus not an implementation of the net procurement function estimated in equations (1) of Table 16. The sensitivity to world price estimated in the equations is added and brings about a large increase in efficiency. A degree of sensitivity to production is included in all of policies 1 through 4—but not in equations (1)—by the existence of a price band. This explains how the fit of equations (2) can be so much better than equations (1), yet policy 5 is no improvement over policy 4.

Policy 6 attempts to correct the shape of the net procurement equation of policy 5 by using the regression results from equations (3a), (3b), and (3c) of Table 16 to allow for different degrees of sensitivity to production and world price over different ranges of production.[30] For all levels of price variability, policy 6 leads to some improvement. The improvement is small, however, ranging from Rs1 million to Rs7 million annually.

The resulting policies are very close in efficiency to the optimal policies. It is thus possible to be confident that policy 6 includes all of the important components of the optimal policy. Indeed, with a price variability of 0.9, policy 6 is actually superior to the "optimal" policy.

Figure 8 explains how this anomaly is possible. Recall that the optimal policies are actually interpolated policies from a discrete optimization process. In the figure, suppose that the truly optimal relationship between production and net procurement is the straight line, but only points on the grid are considered by the discrete optimization procedure. Thus, the points marked with boxes are chosen by the procedure as being superior to all other considered points. These points are the closest points on the grid to the straight line. The interpolated policy will then consist of the grid points and the segments connecting the points. Therefore, a linear regression estimated from the interpolated policy will produce a line that exactly coincides with the truly optimal policy, and a simulation of this policy will produce a superior result to a simulation of the interpolated "optimal" policy.

Although it would be rare for the truly optimal relationship to coincide exactly with the regression results, it is quite possible for the regression line to be closer to the truly optimal relationship than the interpolated policy. This is more likely to be true when the truly optimal relationship loses its curvature as price variability moves toward zero. This explains the anomalous result from Table 17.

---

[30] Tests were conducted modifying policy 4 by allowing the sensitivity of net procurement to world price to be responsive to different levels of production. The resulting policies were no improvement over policy 4.

Figure 7—Net procurement function implied by price band policy

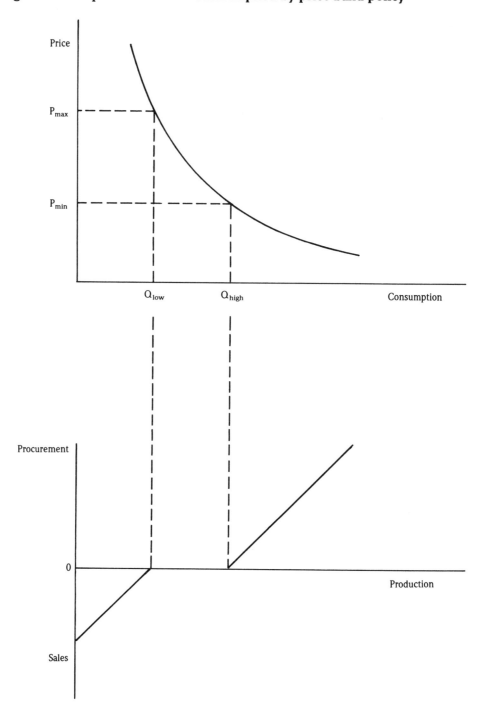

Figure 8—Stylized optimal net procurement function

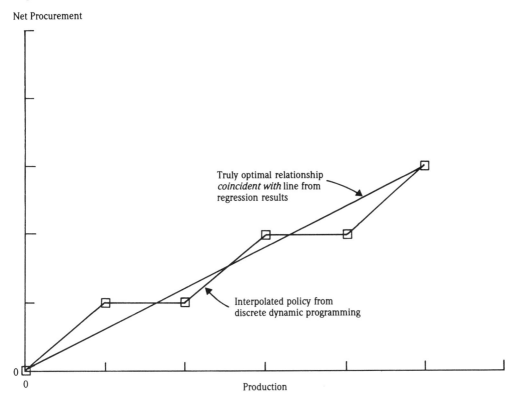

Net Procurement

Truly optimal relationship *coincident with* line from regression results

Interpolated policy from discrete dynamic programming

0

0

Production

Thus, it is possible to delineate the differences between simple price band/buffer stock policies and optimal price, storage, and trade policies. The elements of an efficient policy can be introduced one by one into a price band policy, with the added efficiency of each component measured. The implications of the modeling effort for policy in Pakistan are discussed below.

Policy Implications

The two most important policy recommendations of this analysis are that Pakistan should not hold interannual supply stabilization stocks at present world prices and should not build extra storage capacity for such stocks.

These recommendations are robust for many different changes in assumed parameters, particularly since most parameters were chosen to bias results somewhat toward higher levels of storage. Thus, even though it is impossible to be certain about, say, the amount of food aid Pakistan will receive, even when the extreme assumption of no food aid is made, Pakistan still should not hold interannual stocks.

The savings that accrue from following these recommendations far outweigh the savings for Pakistan that result from modifying the domestic price structure so that it approximates an optimal policy. Nevertheless, there are significant benefits shown in Table 16 and Figure 8, particularly if the government's relative preferences for low fiscal cost and price stability lead to a choice for price variability in the higher range of the tables. Once stock sizes are reduced, the largest gain in efficiency comes from allowing the domestic price to respond to the world price. As pointed out above, the degree of sensitivity is not particularly large, with a US$10 change in the world price leading to a change in the domestic price between Rs0.13 and Rs1.12 per 40 kilograms for the levels of price variability considered here.

World prices are taken into account by the Agricultural Prices Commission in making a recommendation to the government each year. This recommendation, however, is based on September world prices for a crop year that will begin the next April. World prices in dollars can swing widely in seven months; indeed, excluding the large 1972/73 price increase, the standard deviation of the percent changes in the world price from September to April is 80 percent as high as the standard deviation of the percent changes in the annual price.[31] From 1970 to 1987, the range of percent changes in the world price from September to April is from −18 to +32 percent; in 15 out of the 18 years, the absolute change has been larger than US$10 per ton (in 1986 dollars). Because of changes—usually depreciations—in the nominal exchange rate, the world price expressed in rupees can vary even more. Even though these exchange rate changes are to some extent under the control of the government, they are unknown to the agricultural policymakers setting the procurement price.

One way to bring the most recent world price information into the pricing mechanism would be to announce a procurement price at planting time that is calculated assuming a significant fall of 15 percent in the world price. Given the past history of world price changes, it is unlikely that the world price would fall more than this amount between September and April. In mid-April, before procurement begins, the government would announce a "world price bonus payment" to be paid above the procurement price for all wheat procured. The amount of the bonus would be calculated as follows:

$$D = [WP_1 - (0.85 \cdot WP_0)] \cdot S, \tag{14}$$

where

D = world price bonus payment,

WP_0 = world price in September of the last year,

WP_1 = world price on April 15, and

S = sensitivity of the domestic price to the world price.

For example, suppose that the world price in September is US$120 per ton. Given this world price, the government's desired procurement price is Rs85 per 40 kilograms. Suppose also that the government is aiming at a price variability of 5.9, and thus the sensitivity of the domestic price to the world price should be Rs1.120 per US$10 change, or Rs0.112 per US$1 change. Consequently, the procurement price announced at planting time would be

$$85 - 0.112 \cdot (0.15 \cdot 120) = 85 - 2.02 = Rs83,$$

---

[31] U.S. Gulf Port prices for No. 2 hard winter wheat are used in these calculations.

to the nearest 5 paisa.[32] Suppose then that the actual price on April 15 is US$130 per ton. The world price bonus payment to be added to the Rs 83 procurement price would be

$$(130 - 102) \cdot 0.112 = Rs3.15,$$

to the nearest 5 paisa. The total amount paid to farmers would thus be Rs 86.15 per 40 kilograms.

These price movements are not large, yet they lead to significant savings in fiscal cost. If the desired price variability level is lower than 5.9, the degree of sensitivity to world price will be lower still.

The estimates of the savings from allowing the domestic price to be sensitive to domestic production are small. These estimates, however, may not be accurate given Pakistan's present seasonal price policy. The price band policies used in the simulations of policies 1 through 4 assume that the government selling price covers the procurement price plus all incidentals plus the price band. Under such a policy, the average price for the year can vary significantly from year to year. But for this to occur, the price band for even the lowest price variability level would require a selling price more than 50 paisa per kilogram above the procurement price. For 1987/88, this gap was only 8 paisa per kilogram. With such a small gap, the average annual domestic price would be virtually constant from year to year, regardless of the size of production.

If this gap cannot be raised above government costs, the benefits of allowing official prices to be sensitive to domestic prices will be much larger than measured. Sensitivity to production can be built into the system through a bonus payment system, as in the case of sensitivity to world price. A "production bonus payment" could be added to the world price bonus payment. As in the case of the world price bonus payment, the announced procurement price would have to be the lowest price offered under any circumstances. Thus it would be calculated based on the two events that would lower the optimal domestic price: a fall in the world price and an abundant crop.

Suppose, for example, that expected production for next year is 13 million tons. World price in September is US$120 per ton as above. Given the variability of production of 0.06 measured in Chapter 3, the standard deviation of production would be

$$0.06 \cdot 13 \text{ million} = 780,000 \text{ tons.}$$

As in the case of the world price differential, the government wants to announce the lowest price at which it would buy wheat. It consequently assumes high production for the present crop year. A production level of 1.28 standard deviations above the mean would occur about 1 year in 10, while a level 1.64 standard deviations above would occur 1 year in 20. For illustrative purposes, the lower level is chosen. This works out to

$$1.28 \cdot 780,000 = 1 \text{ million tons,}$$

to the nearest 5,000 tons.

As above, suppose that the government's desired procurement price at the world price of US$120 and a production level of 13 million tons is Rs 85 per 40 kilograms.

---

[32] One hundred paisa equal one rupee.

Suppose also that the desired price variability is 5.9 and the government chooses to implement the more complicated, tripartite net purchases function. The regression results from Table 16 indicate that consumption would increase by

$$(1 - 0.471) \cdot 300 + (1 - 0.827) \cdot 700 = 280{,}000 \text{ tons.}[33]$$

This translates into a percentage price change of

$$280/13{,}000/0.3 = 7.2 \text{ percent,}$$

or Rs6.10 per 40 kilograms. Given that the world price adjustment equals Rs2.00, the announced procurement price would be

$$85 - 2 - 6.10 = \text{Rs}76.90 \text{ per 40 kilograms.}$$

Now, assume that the early April forecast of production is 12.9 million tons. This forecast is used to compute the production bonus payment. Although the April forecast will deviate from actual production to some extent, it includes much more information than was known at the time of announcing the procurement price. The bonus payment is then equal to the previously calculated Rs 6.10 (which is what the production bonus payment would equal if production were 13 million tons) plus an adjustment for the shortfall below expected production. The additional change in consumption is

$$(1 - 0.471) \cdot (13.0 \text{ million} - 12.9 \text{ million}) = 53{,}000 \text{ tons.}$$

This amount implies a price change of

$$53/13{,}000/0.3 = 1.36 \text{ percent,}$$

or Rs1.15 to the nearest 5 paisa.

The total production differential is thus $6.10 + 1.15 = \text{Rs}7.25$ per 40 kilograms. The total price paid to farmers is the procurement price plus the production bonus payment plus the world price bonus payment. Assuming the world price bonus payment is Rs3.15 as above, the total payment is

$$76.90 + 3.15 + 7.25 = 87.30.$$

On the other hand, if production had ended up being 14 million tons or more, the production differential would have been zero and the total paid to farmers would have been

$$76.90 + 3.15 = 80.05.$$

---

[33] Since the coefficients are for net procurement, the increase in consumption equals 1 minus (increase in net procurement). The 1-million-ton increase in production is broken down into the first 300,000 tons and the second 700,000 tons because of the partitioning of the net procurement function.

The important point to note here is not the exact calculations, but the existence of sensitivity to domestic production. If the amount of sensitivity shown in these calculations were deemed too large, a lower level of price variability could be chosen (albeit at higher levels of fiscal expenditure). But if the government selling price is to remain below the government cost, some mechanism such as this needs to be instituted to allow a degree of sensitivity of price to production.

In addition, note that both the producer price and the consumer price must respond to the world price and domestic production in order to reap the benefits measured in this chapter. Thus, if a world price bonus payment is added to the procurement price, the government selling price will have to go up by a corresponding amount. Simulations of these policies holding the consumer price constant while the procurement price changes show that virtually all of the benefits disappear.

It is possible to approximate the effect of such price changes on consumption by the poorest households. Although the policies considered here do not significantly change average price across years, it is difficult for the poorest consumers to transfer gains in real income in low-price years to future, high-price years. Indeed, a drop in consumption that leads to death and disease cannot be offset by later increases in income and consumption. And as shown in Mellor 1978, the poor are likely to absorb most of the required change in consumption.

Nevertheless, the income and calorie effects on the poorest groups of the price changes considered here are modest. For the highest level of price variability modeled here—Rs 5.90 per 40 kilograms—in 19 out of 20 years, the change in price would be less than Rs10.00 per 40 kilograms, or 12.5 percent. Since the poorest consumers spend about 12.0 percent of their income on wheat and wheat products, the decline in real income would be about 1.5 percent. If the income elasticity of calorie consumption is 0.5, this implies a reduction in calories of 0.75 percent, or less than 15 calories per person per day.[34] Lower allowable levels of price variability would clearly have an even smaller impact on consumption. Although it is never desirable to decrease incomes of poor people, such a small impact seems unlikely to cause such extreme short-term effects that it cannot be offset by higher incomes in low-price years.

Moreover, the policy conclusions of this report concern the *method* for stabilizing prices more than the *degree* of stability. The government clearly has reasons for stabilizing prices other than consumer welfare. The results presented in this chapter concerning efficient policy design are of relevance regardless of the particular desired level of price stability.

Conclusions

The coefficient of variation of Pakistan's wheat production is about 6 percent. Using stocks to stabilize consumption in the presence of this variability is inefficient unless world prices are less than US$80 per ton. Given any reasonable assumption about future world prices, the value of building additional storage capacity for interannual supply stabilization purposes is much less than the cost. Other than minimizing this

---

[34] This assumes that the decline in calorie consumption results from the decline in real income rather than from the shift in relative prices. In other words, with real income (and thus utility) held constant, poor consumers do not decrease calorie consumption when relative prices change. This would appear to be a reasonable assumption for consumers who already have a calorie deficit.

type of stockholding, the most profitable change in policy would be allowing the domestic price to reflect changes in the world price. This degree of sensitivity is not large, and could be accomplished by paying a "world price bonus payment" above the procurement price. If seasonal price policy, as examined in Chapter 5, does not allow for a release price above government cost, the benefits of allowing the official price to respond to domestic production increase substantially. In that case, a strong rationale exists for instituting a "production bonus payment" also.

5

SEASONAL PRICE POLICY AND STORAGE DEMAND

The previous chapter has analyzed the demand for interannual supply stabilization stocks, the type of storage demand most often analyzed in the literature. The conclusion is that, at the end of the market year, Pakistan should not hold stocks to buffer a possible shortfall in production during the next market year. Thus, one element of storage demand is zero. This does not imply, however, that the government should never hold stocks of any kind. If the government desires to stabilize seasonal price swings, significant stocks could be purchased at harvest time and sold during the remainder of the year. As pointed out in Chapter 2, there is some reason to believe that such within-year stocks for seasonal distribution could be quite large. Thus, it is necessary to analyze the determinants of procurement size and offtake demand in order to assess the total demand for storage in the system.

It is clear that changing the guaranteed procurement price will change the amount procured, holding crop size constant. Less clear, but equally important, is the relationship between the permitted seasonal price rise and procurement size. Holding production and the procurement price constant, the amount of wheat procured by the government will be an inverse function of the allowed seasonal price rise. Showing that this effect is important and measuring its size is the subject of the remainder of this chapter.

The government of Pakistan has only recently begun to cap the seasonal price rise as an alternative to selling wheat through the ration shop system. Early in 1987, the government announced that it was phasing out its ration shop system, which had been in place for more than 40 years. Instead of providing set quantities at a highly subsidized price to a limited segment of the population, the new policy requires the government to sell all that the market will buy at a set price.[35] This change fundamentally alters the relationship of the Pakistan government to the private wheat market.

Historically, the private wheat market has been officially sanctioned and supported by the government, unlike the situation in many less-developed countries where private markets have been tolerated but are in fact illegal. The result has been an active private market in wheat trading. In past years, prices in the private market have shown a marked seasonal pattern, with harvest prices close to the government procurement price, afterward rising an average of 18 percent to a peak in January. Unless the difference between the government buying and selling prices is close to this figure of 18 percent, the expected seasonal price rise would be less. Thus expected returns to storage would be lower than in the past, and private agents consequently would store less. The result would be larger procurement and higher demands on government

---

A version of this chapter entitled "The Effects of Pricing Policy on Seasonal Storage of Wheat in Pakistan" has been submitted for publication in *Agricultural Economics.*

[35] Since most of the supplies earmarked for the ration shops did not reach the intended beneficiaries but were diverted into the open market, the change in policy was not as dramatic as it appears. See Alderman, Chaudhry, and Garcia 1988.

storage facilities. Thus, this topic is of direct relevance to establishing the appropriate size of government storage facilities.

But how important is the private sector in seasonal storage in Pakistan? Does the change in price policy make any substantial difference? What are the implications of this policy in terms of government cost, government procurement, and the growth of private marketing activity?

These questions are addressed in the following way. An examination of the seasonal pattern of prices that have held historically is followed by an estimation of the importance of private-sector seasonal storage. This is followed by the development of a model for examining these issues, using Working's (1949) theory of the price of storage. The model is then estimated, validated, and used to measure fiscal cost, procurement, and private storage under different policy alternatives. Finally, sensitivity analysis and conclusions are presented.

The Historical Seasonal Price Pattern

Figure 9 presents the historical seasonal price pattern, which is constructed using a weighted average of separate price series for Faisalabad, Hyderabad, Lahore, Multan,

Figure 9—Seasonal price rise of wheat in Pakistan, 1979-87

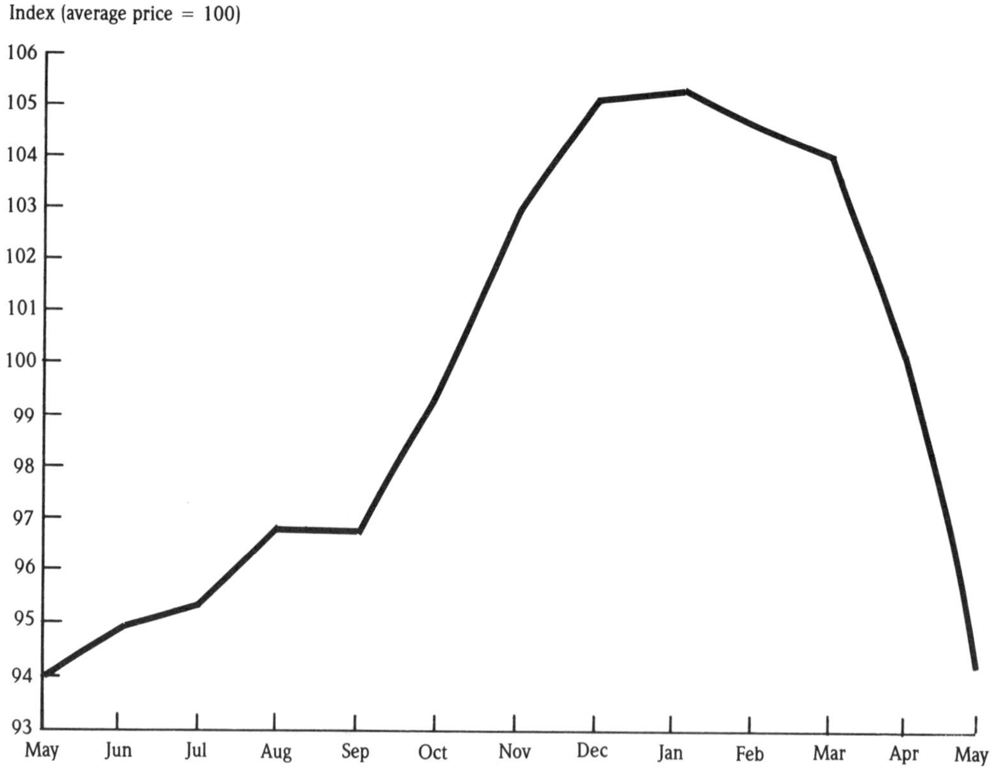

Index (average price = 100)

Source: Data from the Federal Bureau of Statistics, Islamabad.
Note: The price pattern is constructed with a weighted average of separate price series for Faisalabad, Hyderabad, Lahore, Multan, Okara, and Sargodha.

64

Okara, and Sargodha. Since the scale is the average ratio of each month's price to a 12-month moving average, the 12 percent price rise presented in the figure can be considered a real price rise.[36] The figure shows slowly rising prices during the procurement season of May, June, and July, followed by rapid increases in October, November, and December, with prices leveling off before declining dramatically in April and May.

In order to consider nominal prices and the dispersion of price rises across markets and years, Table 18 presents the percentage price rise for each of these six wholesale markets from 1976/77 to 1986/87.[37] In the 10 years prior to 1987, the lowest nominal seasonal price rise in these six markets was 5.3 percent in Hyderabad in 1985/86.[38] The price rise during 1986/87 was considerably smaller, perhaps because the announcement of the policy change was made during the normally high-price months. The rise in market year 1977/78 was exceptionally high, as prices rose dramatically in all markets in the months following the declaration of martial law. Aside from that abnormal year, the highest price rise was 29.8 percent in Okara in 1978/79.

Three-fourths of all the price rises across markets and years from 1978/79 to 1985/86 were between 10 and 25 percent, while price rises greater than 10 percent

Table 18—Seasonal price rises in selected markets, 1976/77-1986/87

Year	Faisalabad	Hyderabad	Lahore	Multan	Okara	Sargodha	Weighted Average
				(percent)			
1976/77	16.5	11.4	9.5	15.6	9.8	17.6	13.1
1977/78	62.3	n.a.	44.3	47.5	58.7	61.9	n.a.
1978/79	13.3	20.5	21.8	24.4	29.8	18.3	22.6
1979/80	12.7	22.6	17.6	7.5	17.7	19.6	14.9
1980/81	10.7	10.2	7.3	5.9	8.9	15.3	8.5
1981/82	22.1	27.3	24.5	20.8	22.7	25.7	23.3
1982/83	14.8	9.4	17.1	17.6	18.5	20.3	16.0
1983/84	18.7	21.1	14.6	17.2	16.4	21.8	17.8
1984/85	18.6	11.1	24.2	27.7	27.6	24.2	22.8
1985/86	18.6	5.3	20.7	15.3	15.4	14.5	14.6
1986/87	6.5	7.1	6.1	6.2	2.7	6.1	5.7
1977-87 average	19.5	n.a.	18.9	18.7	20.8	22.3	n.a.
1979-86 average	16.2	15.9	18.5	17.1	19.6	20.0	17.6

Source: Data from the Federal Bureau of Statistics, Islamabad.
Notes: n.a. means not available. The percentages are derived from prices for the three usually highest-priced months divided by those for the three usually lowest-priced months.

---

[36] The index was developed by constructing a weighted average time series of wholesale prices for the six markets from 1979 to 1987, with the weights determined by average share in total procurement, since this should reflect the extent of wheat available for storage. A seasonal index was then constructed for this weighted average series using the ratio to moving average method. Data from the Federal Bureau of Statistics, Islamabad, were used in the analysis.

[37] To minimize the effects of any single month's data, the table is presented as the percent rise from the three usually lowest-price months (May, June, and July in the Punjab; April, May, and June in the Sind) to the three usually highest-price months (December, January, and February for the Punjab; November, December, and January for the Sind).

[38] The data for Hyderabad for 1977/78 show a price *decline* during a period when the smallest increase in any other market listed here was 44 percent. These data are considered suspect and consequently are not included in the analysis.

occurred 90 percent of the time. Averages by market during this period range from 15.9 percent for Hyderabad to 20.0 for Sargodha. Weighting the price rise for each market by the share of procurement for that market yields an average price rise of 17.6 percent.

In sum, the previous system gave private agents a return to storage that was reasonably secure. Although there is dispersion across markets and years, there was a price rise of 10 percent or more in almost all cases aside from the year in which the new policy was announced.

The Size of Private Storage

The normal seasonal pattern of price rises has given the private sector, particularly surplus farmers, an incentive to store wheat from harvest until the later months in the marketing year. Knowing how much has been stored in different months in different years, however, is difficult, as there have been no national surveys of farmers, traders, and millers that collected such data.

Table 19 presents a monthly time series of minimum estimates of private storage. It was constructed with the aid of the following four assumptions: market arrival of production is assumed to be distributed across months in the same proportion as procurement for each year; losses of 10 percent are incurred at the time of market arrival; private stocks at the end of April from the previous year's harvest are assumed to be zero; and per capita consumption is assumed to be constant across months within a marketing year, with total consumption in the marketing year equal to production less 10 percent, plus offtake from government stocks, minus procurement. These last three assumptions are simplifications that bias the estimate of private stocks downward. The estimate is thus a lower bound for private storage.

Given these assumptions, private storage at the end of any month, PS_t, is equal to private storage at the end of the previous month, PS_{t-1}, plus net production, Q_t, plus offtake, O_t, minus procurement, PC_t, minus consumption, C_t:

$$PS_t = PS_{t-1} + Q_t + O_t - PC_t - C_t. \tag{15}$$

As in the annual model, exports and imports affect private stocks and consumption only through procurement and offtake, since the government controls all foreign trade. The results of applying equation (15) to the monthly data are shown in the last column of Table 19. Private storage is quite large, with 5-6 million tons held at the end of June of each year.

These private stocks are held for at least four purposes. Some traders are holding for later sale; millers are holding for later processing; farmers are holding for later sale; and farmers as well as consumers are holding for own consumption. It would be useful to know how much of this private storage is held for each of these purposes. Unfortunately, this is not possible both because of a lack of microlevel data and because the farmers themselves may shift their intended use depending on prices. The most that can be said about the breakdown is that farmers hold most of the stock at the end of July, since the Agroprogress and Indus (1986) study reports that total storage capacity of traders and millers is only 1.1 million tons.

66

Table 19—Estimated private storage of wheat, 1983-87

Year/Month	Annual Production	Market Arrival of Production	Procure- ment	Offtake	Estimated Private Storage
		(1,000 metric tons)			
1983/84	12,414				
May		4,535	1,551	235	2,570
June		5,106	1,746	147	5,205
July		957	327	146	5,106
August		211	72	179	4,546
September		70	24	181	3,894
October		1	0	217	3,231
November		...	...	263	2,610
December		...	...	316	2,040
January		...	...	385	1,537
February		...	...	399	1,046
March		...	...	420	573
April		452	105	363	388
1984/85	10,882				
May		7,523	1,747	186	5,430
June		1,637	380	172	5,937
July		142	33	227	5,348
August		39	9	243	4,693
September		...	...	266	4,030
October		...	...	285	3,383
November		...	...	306	2,754
December		...	...	366	2,184
January		...	...	441	1,686
February		...	...	397	1,141
March		21	5	431	644
April		1,376	331	372	1,114
1985/86	11,703				
May		7,864	1,892	254	6,399
June		1,023	246	220	6,452
July		229	55	233	5,913
August		21	5	229	5,210
September		...	...	241	4,500
October		...	...	259	3,806
November		...	...	285	3,135
December		...	...	317	2,494
January		...	...	352	1,886
February		...	...	361	1,284
March		17	7	378	707
April		701	282	345	504
1986/87	13,916				
May		7,343	2,952	297	4,279
June		3,473	1,396	231	5,672
July		853	343	247	5,512
August		129	52	244	4,913
September		7	3	255	4,251
October		...	...	265	3,591
November		...	...	276	2,941
December		...	...	311	2,322
January		...	...	351	1,742
February		...	...	347	1,156
March		6	2	432	655
April		921	325	389	702

Source: Author's calculations; data from Federal Bureau of Statistics and Ministry of Food, Agriculture, and Cooperatives, Islamabad.

The Relationship Between Private Storage and Price Rises

The Supply-of-Storage Model

A 12-month model with no uncertainty is used here to estimate the effects of government price policy on private storage in a normal production year. The first several equations parallel those of the interannual model in Chapter 4. Supply, S_t, in any month equals the opening private stocks, PS_t, plus the amount harvested during the month, Q_t, plus offtake from government stocks, O_t:

$$S_t = PS_t + Q_t + O_t, \tag{16}$$

where

$$Q_t = 0 \text{ for } 3 < t < 12.$$

Time, t, equals one in the largest harvest month, May. Harvested amounts, Q_t, are exogenous and equal to zero between August and March. Supply is apportioned between carryout private stocks, PS_{t+1}, consumption, C_t, and government procurement, PC_t:

$$S_t = PS_{t+1} + C_t + PC_t. \tag{17}$$

Consumption is a function of price, P:

$$C_t = f(P_t), \tag{18}$$

while offtake and procurement are functions of price and the release, PR, and procurement, PP, prices. Procurement is zero when the price is above the procurement price, but offtake does not go below a minimal level that is required to support the population in farflung, permanent-deficit areas:

$$PC_t = g_1(PP, P_t), \tag{19}$$

where

$$g_1 = 0 \text{ for } PP < P_t, \text{ and}$$

$$O_t = g_2(PR, P_t), \tag{20}$$

where

$$g_2 = O_{min} \text{ for } PR > P_t.$$

The remaining equation is for the supply of storage. Since this is a certainty model, at time t the expected price for time $t+1$ equals the eventual price at time $t+1$. Therefore, the amount held in storage at time t is a function of the present price and next period's price. In addition, this storage function may shift across months, particularly in an economy with a large number of subsistance producers:

$$PS_t = h_t(P_t, P_{t+1}). \tag{21}$$

Finally, April prices and storage in successive years are assumed to be equal, since this is a certain, normal-production-year model:

$$PS_0 = PS_{12}, \tag{22}$$

$$P_0 = P_{12}. \tag{23}$$

Setting equations (16) and (17) equal to each other and substituting yields:

$$PS_t + Q_t + g_2(PR, P_t) = PS_{t+1} + f(P_t) + g_1(PP, P_t). \tag{24}$$

Using equations (21) through (24), the policy model reduces to a set of 24 nonlinear equations in 24 unknowns: one balance equation and one storage equation for each month.

In applying the model, the demand function is assumed to be constant elasticity with an own-price elasticity of -0.25. This is a reasonable guess for a staple food in a poor country, although some recent estimates are considerably higher (Alderman 1988a). Results are insensitive to the size of this parameter. Prices are calibrated in rupees per 40 kilograms, a standard unit of measure in Pakistan.

The modeling for the supply-of-storage equation is key to producing a reasonable approximation of reality. Most analysts make a distinction between "working" or "pipeline" stocks and "speculative" stocks, with only the latter held sensitive to changes in expected (or futures) prices. Speculative stocks are held only when the expected change in price is greater than the total cost of storage, including physical costs and interest charges (or the appropriate opportunity cost of capital). This is the normal intertemporal arbitrage assumption made, for example, by Lowry et al. (1987) in one of the few interannual storage studies to take seasonal storage into account. The implication of such an assumption for a certainty model is that whenever stocks are held, the price rise equals the cost of storage. The result carries over to models with uncertainty when expectations are rational, as in the Lowry et al. article.

Expected price increases equal to full carrying charges, however, are rarely found empirically. The seasonal price pattern for Pakistan shown in Figure 9, which holds in the presence of large stocks, does not support such a model. Nor is support forthcoming from the large number of studies of futures markets relating the price spread between contracts to the size of stocks (Working 1949; Brennan 1958; Gray and Peck 1981).

Figure 10 presents two stylized versions of the supply-of-storage function, both the general shape found in the empirical studies and the shape that results from the normal intertemporal arbitrage assumption. The key difference is that in Working's formulation, there is no clear distinction between pipeline stocks and speculative stocks. Stockholding is an increasing function of the difference between the expected price (or futures price in most of the empirical work) and the present price, even if the difference is negative. Thus the empirical studies show that if prices are expected to fall in the next month, market actors will hold fewer stocks than if prices are expected to remain constant. The normal intertemporal arbitrage assumption, on the other hand, assumes that private stockholding would be the same in those two circumstances.

Working argues that stockholding is generally not an isolated investment, but part of a larger processing or marketing activity. Stocks have a "convenience yield" or "accessibility value" that increases as total stocks in the economy decrease.

For the purposes of this paper, it is assumed that there is a convenience yield to stocks, and that the shape of the supply-of-storage curve follows that found in the empirical studies. The logarithmic functional form is used. Thus, equation (21) becomes

$$PS_t = (A_t) \exp[B_t(P_{t+1} - P_t)], \tag{25}$$

Figure 10—Stylized supply-of-storage curves

Expected Price Change

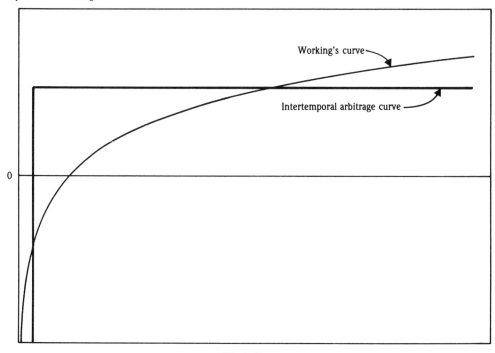

Private Storage

where A_t and B_t are time-specific parameters to be estimated, and exp is the exponential function. See Peck 1977/78 for another use of supply-of-storage curves in the analysis of government stocking schemes.

Estimation of the Model

Two assumptions are necessary in order to estimate the supply-of-storage equation above. First, the expected price change between any two months historically is assumed to equal the average percentage price change between those two months between 1979 and 1987, as shown in Figure 9. Second, it is necessary to assume that either the A parameter or the B parameter in equation (25) is stable across months. The latter option is chosen here, implying that a 1 rupee increase in P_{t+1} leads to the same percentage increase in PS_t, regardless of the value of t, holding P_t constant.

Consequently, there are 13 parameters to estimate from equation (24): 12 values of A (one for each month), and 1 value for B. It is not possible to estimate these simultaneously, however, because the changes in expected price for each month are constant across years, leading to a singular matrix of independent variables in the estimating equation if dummy variables are included for the months. Instead, a two-step procedure is used. First, B is estimated holding A constant; second, the value of A is computed as detailed below.

The estimating equation for B uses data for the logarithm of private storage from July to March of 1979-87 as the dependent variable. April, May, and June are excluded because private storage for those months is more highly variable than for the other nine months, leading to heteroscedasticity. The higher variance in these months results primarily from differences in harvesting time across years and thus would cloud the analysis at hand. The independent variable is the expected price rise. This estimating equation produces an R^2 of 0.61 and a value for B of 0.255 with a t-statistic of 10.5.

Table 20 presents the second-stage, monthly values for the A parameter. These are computed by taking the residuals from the original estimating equation, averaging them for each month, then adding the result to the constant from the equation. The resulting parameters can be interpreted as the amount of storage that will take place each month if there is no expected change in price. Such figures are important, since some modeled policies hold prices close to constant throughout the year. One would expect the values of A to reach a peak in June or July and fall throughout the year until the next harvest begins in April. That general pattern holds, but as Table 20 shows, the estimates for October and November are smaller than the December figure. Consequently, in the policy exercise the constants are adjusted so that

$$A_{t+1} <= A_t \qquad\qquad \text{for } t < 10, \qquad\qquad (26)$$

where $t = 1$ in May. Parameter A is allowed to increase in March and April, with the beginning of the harvest. The revised estimates, presented in column 2 of Table 20, are tested against the original estimates below.

Because a significant component of private storage is for own consumption, private storage is expected to increase with increases in the rural population, holding month and the expected price change constant. In order to test for the influence of rural population on private storage, a second-stage regression was run after adjusting the data series for the monthly values of the A parameter. The effect of this adjustment is to remove the variance in the dependent variable that is correlated with month but uncorrelated with the expected price changes. Consequently, this regression by design had to produce the same value for the B parameter as estimated above. The results are encouraging, with a reasonable elasticity of stocks to rural population of 1.1 and a t-statistic of 7.9. Consequently, the A parameters used in the model—column 3 of Table 20—include an adjustment for the size of the rural population.

Table 20—Parameters for monthly storage equations

Month	Estimated Series	Revised Series	Revised Series Adjusted for Rural Population
		(1,000 metric tons)	
May	2,570	2,570	2,905
June	4,674	4,674	5,283
July	3,549	3,549	4,012
August	4,566	3,549	4,012
September	2,049	2,049	2,316
October	1,325	2,034	2,300
November	1,540	3,034	2,300
December	2,034	2,034	2,300
January	1,930	1,930	2,182
February	1,252	1,252	1,415
March	1,570	1,570	1,775
April	1,920	1,920	2,170

Modeling Government Behavior and Costs

The government sector can be modeled in a straightforward manner. Government procurement and releases are assumed to be proportional to the difference between the actual price and the procurement or release price. Thus, the functional forms for equations (19) and (20) are

$$g_1(PP, P_t) = G(PP - P_t) \qquad \text{for } PP >= P_t \qquad (27)$$
$$= 0 \qquad \text{for } PP < P_t,$$

$$g_2(PR, P_t) = G(P_t - PR) \qquad \text{for } PR <= P_t \qquad (28)$$
$$= O_{min} \qquad \text{for } PR > P_t.$$

The G parameter measures the degree to which the government can defend its price ceiling and floor. It is taken to be 10 million, implying, for example, that procurement would be 2 million tons in a month when market prices are 20 paisa per 40 kilograms below the procurement price. As long as this parameter is large, it has no major effect on the results.

The minimum release parameter, O_{min}, is taken to be 160,000 tons. This equals the lowest figure for offtake per capita in any one month during the last 15 years, adjusted to 1987 population figures. This amount is assumed to be insensitive to price adjustments.

Government expenditure is computed as follows. The costs of buying are assumed to be Rs220 per ton. This includes the cost of bags, delivery charges, fumigation charges, transportation from procurement center to storage center, handling at the storage center, and part of the godown expenses and departmental charges. The costs of selling are assumed to be Rs280 per ton, which includes handling upon removal from storage and transport to the point of sale. Most of this amount is the cost of transporting to and marketing within farflung areas. These numbers are based on figures for incidentals reported by the Pakistan Agricultural Supply and Storage Corporation (PASSCO), the Punjab Food Department, and the Agroprogress and Indus (1986) study. For a more detailed breakdown of the method used to produce these numbers, see Appendix 4.

The government also incurs interest charges on its stock-on-hand of 1.2 percent per month. Physical losses to stock occur at the rate of 0.7 percent per month, or 3.5 percent for a five-month period. This figure is on the low side of studies of losses in government storage reported by Agroprogress and Indus (1986).

The final component of government cost is an adjustment for stock changes during the year. Choosing the appropriate price at which to value the stock is not straightforward, however. Since additional wheat cannot be bought or sold domestically without undermining the stated policy, prevailing domestic prices do not accurately reflect the value of the stock. Consequently, small changes in stock—less than 50,000 tons in a normal production year—are valued at a world price of US$110 per ton. Additions to stock greater than 50,000 tons are valued at the export parity price, since this implies a significant increase in stocks during a normal year. This price is taken here to be US$85 per ton. Similarly, deletions from stocks of more than 50,000 tons are valued at the import parity price of $150 per ton.

Validation of the Model

At this point a complete model of private storage behavior, government market intervention, and government cost structure has been specified. How closely does it model events of the last two years?

Since government policy did not change until March of 1987, present policy is irrelevant to the validation process. However, government offtake and procurement are known for each month during past years, so these figures are treated as exogenous and the model is solved for the endogenous variables: wholesale prices and private storage. Figures 13-16 in Appendix 5 compare the modeled results for endogenous private storage and prices to the historical values of private storage and prices, and to the results using the original A parameters rather than the adjusted A parameter series from Table 20. In each case the adjusted A parameter series is either as good as or superior to the original series. In comparison with the historical values, the fit is good for private storage and reasonably good for prices, considering that the model assumes that no new information enters the market during the year. The 1986/87 actual prices suggest that significant new information did become available between April/May and September/October. Perhaps the actual size of the crop was larger than had been anticipated at harvest time. In any event, the modeled pattern is reasonably good given the inherent instability in seasonal prices.

Results of the Model

The most important results of this model are presented in Table 21. These are discussed below. The first policy tested is the 1987/88 policy. With a crop of 13.4 million tons—an expected "normal" year for Pakistan—the policy of buying wheat at Rs2.00 per kilogram and selling it at Rs2.08 per kilogram is expected to cost Rs3.5 billion per year. Private storage at the end of July is 5.0 million tons. Total procurement under these circumstances is 4.9 million tons, an increase of more than 1.0 million tons compared with expected procurement under the previous policy. Prices reach their maximum in November and remain flat until a small decline in April. Thus there is a marked change in the seasonal price pattern.

Table 21—Implications of width of price band for fiscal cost and private storage

Procurement Price	Release Price	Difference	Fiscal Cost	Procure- ment	Private Storage, July	Private Storage, March	Difference
(Rs/kilogram)		(percent)	(Rs billion)		(million metric tons)		
2.00	2.00	0.0	5.4	7.1	4.2	1.7	2.4
2.00	2.05	2.5	3.9	5.3	4.8	1.5	3.3
2.00	2.08	4.0	3.5	4.9	5.0	1.4	3.7
2.00	2.10	5.0	3.2	4.7	5.2	1.3	3.9
2.00	2.15	7.5	2.6	4.1	5.6	1.0	4.5
2.00	2.20	10.0	2.0	3.6	5.9	0.8	5.0
2.00	2.25	12.5	1.6	3.2	6.1	0.7	5.5
2.00	2.30	15.0	1.3	2.8	6.4	0.6	5.8
2.00	2.40	20.0	0.8	2.2	6.8	0.4	6.4

Source: Author's calculations.

The Rs3.5 billion loss can be broken down into component parts as follows: physical storage losses of 220,000 tons, worth Rs0.6 billion (valued, as argued above, at import parity, since the policy as a whole sells more than it buys domestically); interest charges of Rs0.8 billion; costs of purchasing wheat of Rs1.1 billion; and costs of selling wheat of Rs1.4 billion. This last figure includes about Rs1.0 billion for distributing in the farflung areas, which is the cost of holding prices constant all over the country. The 8 paisa per kilogram difference between buying price and selling price brings the government Rs0.4 billion, thus yielding the Rs3.5 billion cost.

One policy under consideration at the time of derationing was to both buy and sell at Rs2.00 per kilogram. Had this policy been put into effect, the estimated annual cost would have been Rs5.4 billion per year, with procurement rising to 7.1 million tons and private storage in July falling to 4.2 million tons.

The cost savings that resulted from increasing the release price from Rs2.00 to Rs2.08 are much larger than those calculated from multiplying a single offtake figure by the 8 paisa per kilogram gap. With virtually no seasonal price rise, the private sector stores considerably less of the new crop. The increase in private storage from March to July (shown in the last column of Table 21) is more relevant in this context than the July storage figure alone. Because prices decline less in April and May under a flat price policy, private storage is actually *higher* in March and April under this policy, but absorbs considerably less of the harvest than under a policy in which prices are allowed to rise. Thus the government is hit with two large cost increases: the losses per kilogram handled increase because of the lower selling price, and the volume handled increases also. Consequently, losses increase dramatically.

Looked at the other way, losses decline dramatically with only small increases in the release price. Table 21 shows that a 2 paisa increase in the release price from Rs2.08 to Rs2.10 per kilogram is expected to save about Rs300 million per year. Allowing prices to rise 10 percent during the year—the result of making the release price 20 paisa above the procurement price—decreases losses to Rs2.0 billion per year, a savings of Rs1.5 billion annually. And allowing prices to rise 15 percent—a 30 paisa gap—saves Rs2.2 billion annually, with expected costs of Rs1.3 billion per year. As shown in Table 18 and Figure 9, this 15 percent price rise is less than the country has experienced historically.

Figure 11 presents the trade-off curve between price variability and fiscal cost. The horizontal axis is the percent difference between the procurement price and the release price, while the vertical axis is fiscal cost. Clearly there are large savings associated with the first percentage increments of the price differential. The savings that result from raising the gap further grow smaller as the gap grows larger.

The costs considered here are average annual operating costs. Additional savings would result from decreased storage requirements because of lower procurement. Construction costs are about Rs700 million for a million tons of storage (Experience, Zor, and Ferguson 1986). Thus, moving from the 1987/88 policy to one with a 30 paisa gap between procurement and release prices would also save about Rs1.5 billion in construction costs, since procurement declines by 2.1 million tons. This cost is a one-time savings, while the other costs mentioned above are annual savings. A loan for Rs1.5 billion at a 7 percent real interest rate would have an annual payment of about Rs120 million. In addition, 2.1 million tons of storage would have annual fixed costs for maintenance and operating expenses of Rs5-20 million annually. Thus, the total savings of moving from the 1987/88 policy to one with a 30 paisa gap expressed in annual terms would be about Rs2.4 billion annually.

Figure 11—Fiscal cost versus seasonal price band

Annual Fiscal Cost (Rs billion)

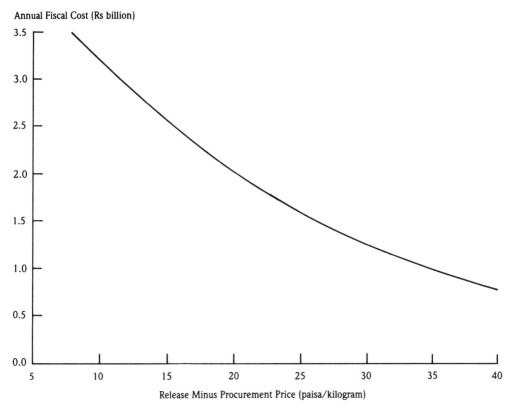

Release Minus Procurement Price (paisa/kilogram)

Sensitivity Analysis

A sensitivity analysis is conducted here for three parameters. The first two parameters check for sensitivity to the specification of the demand equation. The model assumes that if the wholesale price is Rs84, 1 million tons of wheat will be consumed in a month. Values of 82 and 86 are tested here. Second, the own-price demand elasticity is tested. Based on Alderman (1988a), the own-price demand elasticity for wheat in Pakistan is about −0.7, according to the 1979 household and income expenditure survey. This is much larger in absolute value than is normally assumed for a staple food in a poor country. An even larger value of −0.9 is tested below to see if this extreme assumption affects results. Finally, parameter B, the private storage parameter, is tested for values of one standard error above and below its estimated value, taking the standard error from the first-stage estimating equation. Results are presented in Table 22.

The major conclusions do not change at all from these results. The chosen model estimates the cost of 1987/88 policy to be Rs3.47 billion per year and the cost of a policy including a 15 percent price rise to be Rs1.25 billion per year (Table 21, lines 3 and 8. For purposes of comparison, an additional significant digit is reported here.) The range reported in Table 22 is Rs3.40-3.54 billion for 1987/88 policy and Rs1.15-1.38 billion for a 15 percent price rise. The largest difference in estimated savings that result from increasing the width of the price differential to 15 percent is about Rs0.10 billion.

Table 22—Sensitivity analysis

Procurement Price	Release Price	Fiscal Cost	Procure- ment	Private Storage, July	Private Storage, March	Difference
(Rs/kilogram)		(Rs billion)		(million metric tons)		
Equilibrium Price = Rs82/40 Kilograms						
2.00	2.08	3.45	5.0	5.0	1.4	3.7
2.00	2.20	2.01	3.6	5.9	0.8	5.0
2.00	2.30	1.29	2.8	6.4	0.6	5.8
Equilibrium Price = Rs86/40 Kilograms						
2.00	2.08	3.49	4.9	5.1	1.4	3.7
2.00	2.20	2.04	3.6	5.9	0.8	5.0
2.00	2.30	1.24	2.8	6.4	0.6	5.8
Demand Elasticity = −0.9						
2.00	2.08	3.48	4.8	5.1	1.4	3.7
2.00	2.20	1.95	3.5	5.9	0.8	5.0
2.00	2.30	1.38	2.8	6.3	0.6	5.8
B Parameter 1 Standard Error Higher						
2.00	2.08	3.40	4.8	5.1	1.3	3.8
2.00	2.20	1.92	3.4	6.0	0.8	5.2
2.00	2.30	1.15	2.6	6.5	0.5	6.0
B Parameter 1 Standard Error Lower						
2.00	2.08	3.54	5.0	5.0	1.4	3.6
2.00	2.20	2.14	3.8	5.8	0.9	4.9
2.00	2.30	1.36	3.0	6.2	0.6	5.6

Source: Author's calculations.

Consequently, these results are considered to be robust. Actual costs in any particular year, however, could vary significantly from those reported here, especially because of deviations from normal production. In addition, the costs reported here are those associated with the policy after private stocks have adjusted to their new desirable level given the policy change. In the first years after a policy change, stock adjustments could significantly affect cost. Finally, as in any econometric exercise using estimated parameters, the further one moves from the policy under which the estimation took place, the less reliable are the results. Thus, results for price changes on the order of 10-20 percent should be considered more reliable than those with virtually no price change.

Conclusions

The benefits of raising the release price are clear. Savings of approximately Rs2 billion were realized from the government decision to release wheat at Rs2.08 per kilogram rather than Rs2.00 per kilogram. Significant additional reductions in cost will result from the wider band implemented for 1988/89.

The primary savings come from increasing private-sector storage. This study has only considered the benefits of increasing storage by increasing seasonal price changes, but there may be other ways the government could encourage such activity. Since more than 80 percent of private storage in July is on-farm, such storage has to be the primary focus of any such efforts. One obvious change would be to remove from the books the laws that allow the District Food Controller to force the sale of stocks of wheat to a specified agent at a specified price (Agroprogress and Indus 1986). Even if this power is not used, the presence of such laws on the books inhibits private storage.

The costs to the consumer of raising the release price are moderate. These can be estimated as in Chapter 4. If the government were to release wheat at Rs2.30 per kilogram, that price would be effective only during the months of December, January, and February according to the model, because private traders would undersell the government prior to December. Thus the average increase in wheat price would be only about 6.00 percent rather than the 11.00 percent increase from Rs2.08 to Rs2.30 per kilogram.[39] The average consumer spends about 8.00 percent of annual household income on wheat and wheat products. Thus, the real income loss associated with a 6.00 percent price rise is less than 0.50 percent. The poorest consumers, who spend about 12.00 percent of income on wheat and wheat products, would suffer an income loss for the year of less than 0.75 percent.

Nevertheless, the income loss is not spread out evenly over the months, and for the three months in which the maximum price is in effect the real income loss for the poorest consumers is $(0.11 \cdot 0.12)$ or 1.3 percent. If the income elasticity for calorie consumption is 0.5, this would imply a reduction in calorie consumption during those months of 0.6-0.7 percent, or about 15 calories per day. Although it is undesirable to reduce the income of the poorest group, it seems clear that a program that costs Rs2.3 billion annually to raise calorie consumption of the poorest groups by only 15 calories per day for only three months of the year is inefficient. Assuming that the poorest quartile of the population is the target group, the cost works out to approximately Rs1.00 for every 20 additional calories during the three high-priced months. Since Rs1.00 can buy about 1,500 calories, the inefficiency of the policy is obvious. The more efficient policy calls for government intervention in extreme circumstances, thus averting disastrous price rises, but allows for private marketing at most other times.

Another way to view the loss to consumers is to compare costs under a 15 percent change in official prices to those under the old system. As shown above, the average price rise under the old system was 15-20 percent, with some years substantially higher. Although the ration shop price was constant throughout the year, very little was actually being sold at the subsidized price (Alderman, Chaudhry, and Garcia 1988). Consequently, under a policy with a 15 percent price cap, the consumer would be no worse off than under the old system, and in some years substantially better off.

Thus, the model presented here allows for the measurement of trade-offs between cost and seasonal price stability. For the wider purposes of this study, the relationship between seasonal price policy and the demand for storage is important. Chapter 6 examines the final source of storage demand, import buffer stocks, and Chapter 7 aggregates the demand for storage from the three different sources.

---

[39] The 6 percent figure is calculated by taking the average of the percentage increases by month as estimated by the model, weighting each month equally. Since one would expect higher consumption of wheat in low-price months, this estimate of the average price increase is on the high side. Graphs of single years of data in the Agroprogress and Indus (1986) report indicate that the price rise is similar for retail flour and wholesale wheat.

6

OTHER STORAGE REQUIREMENTS

Stocks for Smooth Functioning During Normal Periods

The third and final component of storage after interannual supply stabilization and seasonal stocks consists of amounts required to maintain the normal functioning of the market. This component can be broken down further into two subcomponents: the amount necessary during normal periods of operation, and the amount necessary to disburse after imports have been ordered but before they arrive in the country. This section estimates the former amount.

One way to approach this estimation is to examine past stock levels relative to offtakes. If no disruptions in supply occurred when stocks were at low levels, these historical amounts can be considered upper limits for the amount required to ensure normal operations. Because of the seasonal stocks the government has held in the past, the lowest stock levels have occurred at the beginning of April and May, immediately prior to the procurement season.

Stocks on May 1 have been less than offtake during May in 6 out of the last 18 years. Indeed, in May of 1970, 1972, 1974, 1975, and 1978, opening stocks were less than one-half of May offtake. In several of those years, the stocks held on April 1 were also less than offtake during April. Stocks have always been larger than offtake since 1978; nevertheless, the past history of lower stock levels indicates that if opening stocks are equal to expected offtakes in a given month, it is unlikely that supply disruptions will occur.

In planning for this component of storage, then, it is necessary to have an estimate of expected offtakes by month. The move away from the ration shop system has changed the nature of private-sector demand for government offtakes, thus past patterns may not be accurate indicators of the future. Nevertheless, in the last 10 years the ration shop system has moved away somewhat from a distribution of set quantities and toward meeting demand, at least partly because of the illegal diversion of supplies from the ration shops. Until more data become available on behavior since the policy change, these past patterns will be the most reliable indicators of the seasonality of demand for government supplies.

Since the pattern of offtakes took on a much more marked seasonal pattern after 1975/76, the period 1976/77-1986/87 will be considered. Past data are put in per capita terms to allow comparisons across years. Table 23 presents these offtake data for the individual months and averages over the time period. In addition, the standard deviation, maximum, and minimum are presented for each month. The last column presents aggregate data for the market year.

Over the 11 years in the table, offtakes per capita have averaged slightly over 36 kilograms per capita per year. There is no apparent trend in the data. The first seven months of the market year—May through November—all have averages under 3 kilograms, while December through April all have averages above 3 kilograms. Indeed, for the last four months of the market year, the minimum observed offtake per capita is greater than 3 kilograms. January, February, and March are the highest offtake months.

Table 23—Offtake per capita, by month, May 1976-April 1987

Scheme Year	May	June	July	August	September	October	November	December	January	February	March	April	Annual Total
							(kilograms)						
1976/77	2.55	2.46	2.25	2.60	2.14	2.27	2.64	3.14	3.87	4.65	4.72	4.00	37.3
1977/78	2.89	2.68	2.63	2.55	2.43	2.80	3.10	3.68	4.01	3.63	3.87	3.51	37.8
1978/79	2.93	2.89	2.94	3.05	2.71	3.03	2.97	3.40	3.58	3.51	3.60	3.33	37.9
1979/80	2.79	2.51	2.59	2.38	2.61	2.65	2.44	2.68	3.11	3.34	3.54	3.27	33.9
1980/81	2.70	2.55	2.47	2.23	2.37	2.34	2.71	2.98	3.28	3.18	3.24	3.14	33.2
1981/82	2.80	2.48	1.67	1.71	1.90	2.40	3.28	3.85	4.29	4.21	4.76	3.98	37.3
1982/83	2.64	1.93	1.63	2.05	2.23	2.72	3.06	3.51	3.91	3.74	3.88	3.80	35.1
1983/84	2.61	1.63	1.61	1.97	1.99	2.38	2.88	3.45	4.19	4.33	4.55	3.92	35.5
1984/85	2.01	1.85	2.44	2.60	2.84	3.03	3.25	3.88	4.66	4.18	4.53	3.90	39.2
1985/86	2.65	2.29	2.42	2.37	2.49	2.67	2.93	3.25	3.60	3.69	3.85	3.51	35.7
1986/87	3.01	2.34	2.49	2.46	2.56	2.65	2.76	3.10	3.49	3.44	4.27	3.84	36.4
Average	2.69	2.33	2.28	2.36	2.39	2.63	2.91	3.36	3.82	3.81	4.07	3.65	36.3
Standard deviation	0.26	0.36	0.43	0.35	0.28	0.25	0.25	0.35	0.44	0.45	0.50	0.30	1.73
Maximum	3.01	2.89	2.94	3.05	2.84	3.03	3.28	3.88	4.66	4.65	4.76	4.00	39.2
Minimum	2.01	1.63	1.61	1.71	1.90	2.27	2.44	2.68	3.11	3.18	3.24	3.14	33.2

Source: Collected from the Ministry of Food, Agriculture, and Cooperatives, data originate from the provincial food departments.

The highest offtake per capita in any one month occurred in March of 1982, 4.76 kilograms, while the lowest occurred in July of 1983, 1.61 kilograms.

Thus, it is clear that large numbers of persons rely on their own stocks or stocks from private traders during the first several months of the year, and then begin to depend on the government later in the year. Since average monthly per capita consumption is about 10 kilograms, the government is supplying about 40 percent of total consumption in March, but only about 20 percent in July.

The amount required for normal periods of operation, then, has a marked seasonal component. Multiplying the average per capita offtake figures by present population yields a requirement at the beginning of May of about 280,000 tons. For March, the figure is about 430,000 tons. As stated above, these should be considered upper limits, subject to change as more data become available from the postrationing era.

Import Buffer Stocks

Besides the stocks required for normal operations, there is a requirement for wheat to sell during the lag between ordering and receipt of imports. Normally it is assumed that imports take three months to arrive. This analysis will assume that four months are required from the time imports are ordered until that wheat is available for general distribution in the country.[40] Past patterns can also be useful here to examine how much government stocks have been depleted in any given four-month period.

The first step in the analysis is to take the data in Table 23 and aggregate it over four-month periods. This is done in Table 24, which presents four-month aggregates of per capita offtakes. In this case, the June-September period is the lowest offtake period at 9.36 kilograms per capita, while the January-April period is the highest at 15.35 kilograms. The maximum four-month offtake during the last 11 years was January-April 1985 at 17.27 kilograms per capita, and the minimum was June-September of 1983 at 7.21 kilograms.

Offtakes alone, however, overestimate the required import buffer stock. Even in a bad year, significant amounts are procured from surplus areas during April, May, June, and July. Table 25 adds procurement for the same four-month periods to the offtakes and presents the net offtake in each period.

Since procurement is considerably more variable than offtake, the standard deviations in Table 25 are much larger than those in Table 24. The maximum four-month period for net offtakes is December-March, with an average of 15.04 kilograms per capita, whereas the minimum is April-July at −21.89 kilograms per capita. April-July of 1986 had the lowest net offtake on the table at −39.01 kilograms, while December-March 1985 had the highest at 17.19.

It is of special interest that all of the numbers in Table 25 for March-June, April-July, and May-August are negative; moreover, in all the years after the 1978 rust attack, the smallest number (in absolute value) for these three periods is −11.71 kilograms per capita (for March-June of 1984). This implies that in all of these four-month periods, government stocks ended the period at higher levels than they began (ignoring any imports or exports that may have taken place). There is thus no need to order imports

---

[40] In the rare case when a ship is delayed longer than this period of time, it is possible in the international wheat market to pay a premium in order to divert a ship bound for another port to Karachi. Such occurrences should be infrequent enough that this excess cost can be ignored.

Table 24—Cumulative per capita offtakes: four-month aggregates, 1976/77-1986/87

Scheme Year	May-August	June-September	July-October	August-November	September-December	October-January	November-February	December-March	January-April	February-May	March-June	April-July
						(kilograms)						
1976/77	9.85	9.44	9.25	9.65	10.19	11.92	14.30	16.37	17.24	16.26	14.29	12.20
1977/78	10.75	10.29	10.41	10.88	12.01	13.59	14.42	15.19	15.03	13.95	13.21	12.27
1978/79	11.81	11.59	11.72	11.76	12.11	12.98	13.46	14.08	14.01	13.22	12.22	11.21
1979/80	10.26	10.09	10.23	10.08	10.38	10.88	11.57	12.67	13.26	12.85	12.06	10.99
1980/81	9.95	9.63	9.42	9.66	10.40	11.31	12.14	12.67	12.83	12.35	11.66	10.08
1981/82	8.65	7.76	7.68	9.29	11.43	13.82	15.63	17.11	17.25	15.59	13.32	10.19
1982/83	8.25	7.84	8.63	10.05	11.52	13.20	14.22	15.04	15.33	14.03	11.92	9.65
1983/84	7.83	7.21	7.96	9.22	10.69	12.90	14.85	16.52	16.99	14.81	12.33	10.21
1984/85	8.89	9.73	10.91	11.72	13.00	14.82	15.97	17.25	17.27	15.27	13.38	11.27
1985/86	9.74	9.58	9.96	10.47	11.35	12.46	13.48	14.40	14.65	14.06	12.71	11.35
1986/87	10.30	9.85	10.16	10.43	11.07	12.00	12.78	14.30	15.03	13.99	13.44	11.94
Average	9.66	9.36	9.67	10.29	11.29	12.72	13.89	15.05	15.35	14.21	12.77	11.03
Standard deviation	1.11	1.22	1.17	0.83	0.82	1.10	1.31	1.54	1.56	1.13	0.77	0.86
Maximum	11.81	11.59	11.72	11.76	13.00	14.82	15.97	17.25	17.27	16.26	14.29	12.27
Minimum	7.83	7.21	7.68	9.22	10.19	10.88	11.57	12.67	12.83	12.35	11.66	9.65

Source: Collected from the Ministry of Food, Agriculture, and Cooperatives, data originate from the provincial food departments.

Table 25—Cumulative per capita net offtakes: four-month aggregates, 1976/77-1986/87

Scheme Year	May-August	June-September	July-October	August-November	September-December	October-January	November-February	December-March	January-April	February-May	March-June	April-July
					(kilograms)							
1976/77	-19.41	-11.32	1.36	7.42	9.02	11.29	14.04	16.35	16.85	8.08	-4.72	-10.51
1977/78	-12.70	-5.86	4.95	9.12	11.37	13.44	14.42	15.19	14.55	5.61	-0.20	-1.58
1978/79	-1.68	5.93	11.11	11.59	12.06	12.95	13.46	14.08	13.46	0.16	-12.69	-17.13
1979/80	-18.20	-6.53	5.41	8.69	9.67	10.83	11.57	12.67	12.40	-6.38	-21.01	-24.16
1980/81	-24.80	-7.00	6.59	8.91	10.13	11.28	12.14	12.67	10.94	-13.30	-31.50	-35.93
1981/82	-36.18	-13.57	3.84	8.30	11.14	13.78	15.60	17.09	16.12	4.29	-16.64	-24.87
1982/83	-26.31	-16.63	2.81	9.34	11.44	13.20	14.22	15.04	14.22	-4.31	-25.77	-31.65
1983/84	-33.15	-16.81	3.28	8.16	10.43	12.89	14.85	16.52	15.86	-5.15	-11.71	-14.18
1984/85	-14.46	5.19	10.46	11.63	13.00	14.82	15.97	17.19	13.75	-8.02	-12.48	-15.10
1985/86	-13.21	6.40	9.34	10.42	11.35	12.46	13.48	14.32	11.71	-18.80	-34.26	-39.01
1986/87	-37.71	-8.28	6.15	9.88	11.04	12.00	12.78	14.28	11.81	-10.00	-23.53	-26.68
Average	-21.62	-6.23	5.94	9.40	10.97	12.63	13.87	15.04	13.79	-4.35	-17.68	-21.89
Standard deviation	10.67	8.22	3.06	1.30	1.06	1.15	1.30	1.54	1.86	7.91	10.18	10.84
Maximum	-1.68	6.40	11.11	11.63	13.00	14.82	15.97	17.19	16.85	8.08	-0.20	-1.58
Minimum	-37.71	-16.81	1.36	7.42	9.02	10.83	11.57	12.67	10.94	-18.80	-34.26	-39.01

Source: Collected from the Ministry of Food, Agriculture, and Cooperatives, data originate from the provincial food departments.

between March and June; by the time the imports arrived, government stocks would be higher than when they were ordered.

The import buffer component of government stocks for February, March, and April, therefore, simply needs to be enough to bridge the gap until procurement comes on line at the end of the market year. From June to January, however, there is a need for stocks in case imports are required. These needs should be based on the highest observed offtake per capita over each four-month period, since offtakes are likely to be on the higher end of the scale in deficit years.

Therefore, month-by-month storage requirements for these two components are as reported in Table 26. The absolute amounts are computed by multiplying the per capita figures by 105 million persons. The monthly required stock—column 5 of the table—is the larger of either the import buffer or the amount required for normal operations, since the import buffer stocks can also fulfill the normal operations role. The import buffer is the larger of the two in all months except May.

The monthly required stock shown in column 5, then, is the minimum amount of wheat with which the government should begin any month. If opening stocks for any month are below the amount shown in this column, imports should be ordered if there is enough time for them to arrive before procurement begins. During March and April and to some extent in February, it is unlikely that imports could be ordered, received, and distributed before the country is again in surplus. Consequently, for these months the numbers are reference points that can be used as targets in earlier months rather than import triggers.

The required stocks peak in December and drop off only slightly in January. It is clear that if the January requirement is going to be met without imports, then all previous targets will be met also. The subsequent targets will be met, too, unless offtakes per capita increase to levels above the historical maximum. Based on this observation, the last column in Table 26 shows the amount of stock required at the beginning of each month to ensure that the January target is met if net offtakes per capita follow the average historical pattern. For January and subsequent months, the column is equal to the required stock column. The export trigger column peaks in

Table 26—Storage requirements for normal operations and import buffer

Month	Import Buffer		Normal Operations		Monthly Required Stock	Minimum Amount to Trigger Exports
	Per Capita	Absolute	Per Capita	Absolute		
	(kilograms)	(1,000 metric tons)	(kilograms)	(1,000 metric tons)	(1,000 metric tons)	
May	0.0	0	2.69	282	282	650
June	6.4	672	2.33	245	672	2,040
July	11.1	1,167	2.28	239	1,167	3,047
August	11.6	1,221	2.36	248	1,221	3,108
September	13.0	1,365	2.39	251	1,365	2,920
October	14.8	1,556	2.63	276	1,556	2,694
November	16.0	1,677	2.91	306	1,677	2,424
December	17.2	1,805	3.36	353	1,805	2,121
January	16.9	1,769	3.82	401	1,769	1,769
February	13.4	1,404	3.81	400	1,404	1,404
March	8.7	918	4.07	427	918	918
April	4.0	420	3.65	383	420	420

Source: Author's calculations.

August at 3.1 million tons. If early August stocks are above this amount and world prices are such that interannual supply stabilization stocks are uncalled for, the amount in excess of 3.1 million could be exported without fear that imports would be required during the present market year. These numbers, then, are the minimum figures that the government would want to use as export triggers.

This last column in the table also provides the maximum storage space requirement for these components. If the government had only enough space for the monthly required stock, it could not store sufficient quantities from the previous harvest to meet the required stock amounts for January. Thus, storage requirements to ensure normal operations must be at least 3.1 million tons, with the amount peaking in early August.

These calculations are based on past data, with some weight placed on the highest historical observations of offtake per capita. Actual requirements for monthly offtake will depend to a significant extent on the gap between the procurement and release price, discussed in Chapter 5. In particular, should the government increase the gap significantly, private stocks may play a more important role, and thus stocks required for import buffer and normal operations may decrease. In addition, during the years when these past data were produced, the government was not promising to sell all that was demanded at a set price. If the government convinces private agents that it will sell whatever is demanded and arrange for imports in a timely manner when necessary, speculative runs will be avoided. Since there was no maximum price under the old system, there was more incentive to hoard grain during a time of perceived scarcity. Thus, per capita offtake, and consequently stock requirements, during the deficit years in Table 25 should be an upper limit to net demand for government stocks under present policy.

In sum, the demand for stocks to maintain the normal functioning of the market is highly seasonal. Amounts required to buffer import arrival are the most seasonal, but requirements for normal operations also have a significant seasonal component. Total storage requirements can only be estimated on a monthly basis because of this highly seasonal nature. The maximum required storage capacity in any one month for the components measured in this chapter is 3.1 million tons; this estimate, which is based on historical data, is thought to be on the high side given recent policy changes.

7

CONCLUSIONS

Total Requirement for Government Storage Facilities

Previous chapters have measured the requirements for government storage from the three different sources: interannual supply stabilization stocks, seasonal storage, and stocks to ensure a continuous supply of wheat under all circumstances. This chapter combines the results from the different analyses in order to calculate the total demand for public storage of wheat. Interannual supply stabilization stocks do not appear in this analysis, since Chapter 4 shows that it is unprofitable to build additional capacity for such stocks.

Government storage capacity will be equal to required size of stock in the highest demand month in a year of abundant supply. Thus, in order to estimate total demand for public storage, it is necessary to compare demand for storage space for procurement in a high-production year with the monthly stock requirements for normal operations, import buffer, and minimum export trigger from Table 26. Clearly, if the demand for space for procurement is above the highest value of the minimum export trigger, required storage capacity for the export trigger will be satisfied if sufficient space for procurement is available.

Before such a comparison is made, however, it is necessary to translate the annual procurement figures from Chapter 5 into monthly requirements for storage space. To accomplish this, the percentage of total procurement that took place in each month is calculated for buying years 1984-87. The chosen starting year is 1984 because the procurement season apparently shifted to somewhat earlier dates beginning with that year. Ignoring the small amounts of procurement in March, August, and September, the percentage of procurement that has taken place in April, May, June, and July is approximately 8, 63, 24, and 5 percent, respectively.

Expected procurement in April is less than expected offtake. Therefore, the opening stocks in May assumed in the calculation of the procurement storage requirement is the minimum export trigger for May from Table 26, 650,000 tons. If opening stocks are larger than this amount and the crop is abundant, exports can be arranged immediately. Total requirements for May are therefore 650,000 tons plus 63 percent of procurement less expected offtake in May. The June requirement replaces the 650,000-ton opening stock with the calculated figure for closing stocks in May.

Total annual procurement must also be assumed in order to calculate specific storage requirements. As shown in previous chapters, procurement will vary with both crop size and the gap between procurement and release prices. Procurement in a normal production year for any given gap between procurement and release prices is presented in Table 21. Since this analysis is for maximum public storage requirements under a particular price policy, however, these levels of procurement must be adjusted upward for good crop years.

These adjustments can be made in the following manner. Elsewhere it has been estimated that an increase in production of 100,000 tons leads to an increase in procurement of about 84,000 tons (Pinckney 1988c). The percentage is much higher than the average share of production procured—about 30 percent—because two factors are working together. First, virtually all of the increase in production in an exceptionally good year is marketed surplus, while a large percentage of a normal crop is consumed on-farm. Second, the increase in marketed surplus leads to a decline in the wholesale price, causing procurement to consume a larger percentage of marketed surplus.

The 84 percent marginal rate can be applied to the expected increase in production in a good year. Clearly the size of the increase depends on how unusual the year is. With a standard deviation of production of 6 percent (see Chapter 3), a crop 10 percent above trend would be expected to occur only once every 20 years. Ten percent of the 1987/88 normal year production level is about 1.3 million tons; 84 percent of that amount is about 1.1 million tons. Thus, a figure of 1.1 million tons needs to be added to the normal production year procurement in order to account for demand for storage from procurement in an exceptionally good year.

Therefore, with a 20 paisa gap between the procurement and release prices, total procurement in an exceptional year would be $3.6 + 1.1 = 4.7$ million tons. This total annual procurement is apportioned by month and adjusted for offtakes in Figure 12. Calculations are made below both for a gap of 8 paisa—the 1986/87 gap—and for a gap of 30 paisa or 15 percent—the approximate historical seasonal price rise.

Although total procurement is 4.7 million tons, total storage requirements never reach this level because of offtakes during the buying season. The curve for the storage of high-production-year procurement peaks in June and July at 4.2 million tons. As this amount is above the 3.1-million-ton peak of the minimum export trigger line, there

Figure 12—Total storage requirements: 20 paisa seasonal gap

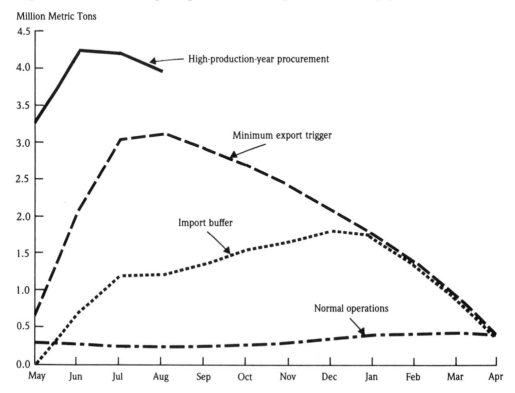

would always be sufficient capacity for normal operations and import buffer if there is sufficient capacity for high-production-year procurement. Therefore, 4.2 million tons would be the required storage capacity of the government for wheat if the gap between the procurement and release prices is 20 paisa.

As pointed out in Chapter 5, however, the appropriate storage capacity of the government is a function of price policy. If the government were to institute a gap of 30 paisa per kilogram between the procurement and release prices, expected procurement in an excellent production year would be 3.9 million tons. Under this scenario, requirements peak in June at 3.5 million tons, or 700,000 tons below requirements when the price gap is 20 paisa per kilogram. This is still above the 3.1 million minimum export trigger. Similarly, if the policy for 1987/88 had been continued so that there was only an 8 paisa gap, expected procurement after a bumper crop would be 6.0 million tons, with peak requirements of 5.4 million tons in July.

Thus, government storage requirements for wheat at present are 3.5-5.4 million tons, assuming that the gap between procurement and release prices is between 8 and 30 paisa per kilogram. The projections in Chapter 3 suggest that wheat production will increase at a rate of approximately 3.3 percent annually. This implies that required storage capacity of the government will have to rise to between 5.3 and 8.2 million tons by the year 2000, with the exact point determined by price policy.

Policy Implications

Policy changes implied by this analysis have been discussed throughout the report. These include
- Choosing a gap between procurement and release price that takes account of the large cost savings both from lower annual subsidies and reduced future storage requirements;
- Allowing the official domestic price to respond to changes in production by introducing a production bonus system after choosing an appropriate level of variability of interannual domestic prices;
- Holding no interannual supply stabilization stocks; and
- Allowing the domestic price to reflect changes in the world price.

The most important of these policy adjustments is the gap between the procurement and release prices. Chapter 5 shows that a 2 paisa increase in this gap from its 1987/88 level saves Rs300 million annually (about US$17 million), with cost savings for reduced storage requirements above this amount. Over a wider range, this tool has the potential to save the government billions of rupees annually.

If the gap between the procurement and release prices remains smaller than government marketing costs, the second intervention to consider is introducing the production bonus payment system as outlined in Chapter 4. The key to having an efficient interannual supply stabilization policy is allowing average domestic prices to vary somewhat from year to year, depending on the crop size and the government's desired trade-off between price variability and fiscal cost. The average annual price will change very little as long as the gap is less than marketing costs. Introducing a production bonus payment—even a very small one—could decrease costs by about 100 million rupees annually.

Of equal importance to introducing a production bonus payment is lowering interannual supply stabilization stocks to zero unless the world price plummets to unprecedented depths. This change also saves about 100 million rupees annually, depending on the exact level of stock reduction. If the government is to lower interannual supply stabilization stocks to zero, however, it is necessary to ensure the availability of foreign exchange for imports when supplies are short. This should not be a problem, as the analysis clearly shows that the average supply of foreign exchange is higher under a policy with low stocks than under one with large stocks. Nevertheless, there are individual years when large imports will be necessary. The IMF Compensatory Financing Facility, discussed in Appendix 6, is one possible source of foreign exchange in such years.

The next most important policy adjustment would be to allow official prices to reflect changes in the world price between September and April by instituting a world price bonus payment system. This would save about Rs 30 million annually, depending on the overall degree of price variability.

The final policy change suggested here is to change the law concerning the ability of government agents to seize private stores in an emergency. The payoff from this change is unmeasurable, but any increase in other incentives will decrease the seasonal price increase required to induce the private sector to store a given amount of grain, and will thus lower the cost to the government of any particular seasonal price policy. Given the high responsiveness of fiscal cost to the size of the gap, the payoff from a policy change such as this is likely to be large.

Thus, the policy adjustments considered here all move toward making Pakistan's wheat policy more sensitive to uncontrollable parameters, such as weather-induced fluctuations in crop size and changes in the world price. The most efficient way to create this sensitivity is to encourage more private-sector involvement in seasonal storage by increasing the price incentive and removing the legal disincentive, and to implement some sensitivity of official prices to outside forces. Interannual government stocks are an inefficient way to stabilize supplies.

In the interannual context, however, it is very important that the government actually sell all that is demanded at its ceiling price, whatever that price may be. As long as private agents expect the government to defend its price, there is no incentive to attempt to hoard, since there will be no returns to hoarding. On the other hand, if private agents sense that the government is holding back on supplies, there could be a costly run on government stocks. Even in this situation—rather, especially in this situation—it is vital that the government sell sufficient quantities to meet demand, importing all that is necessary to do so. In the long run, consistency in meeting demand will be cheaper than restricting supplies because of the expectations formed that the government will always defend its price.[41]

Thus, if the government is concerned about lowering fiscal cost, ensuring supplies for the market, and allowing the growth of private marketing activities, increasing the gap between the procurement price and the release price should be the first priority. Next, lowering interannual supply stabilization stocks and introducing some response of official prices to production size should be considered. Adding sensitivity to the world price would lower costs further. Finally, removing the legal impediments to private storage would have an unmeasurable benefit that could be large.

Implications for Other Countries

Pakistan presents a particularly interesting case for analyzing the demand for storage because of the recent change in marketing policy there. Some conclusions—such as

---

[41] See Siamwalla 1988 for a discussion of the importance of this factor in the success of Indonesia's storage, trade, and price policy for rice.

the inefficiency of building any additional storage for supply stabilization stocks and the relative benefits of different policy modifications—will not carry over to other countries. The general pattern of policy changes that will lead to more efficient price, storage, and trade policies, however, will be similar for other countries that are normally self-sufficient in a staple food.

The need to analyze separately the three components of storage demand has been brought out clearly. Although interannual stocks should be zero for Pakistan at present world prices, some countries should hold stocks across years when surpluses exist. The following changes in parameters will increase the average size of efficient interannual stocks.

1. Higher production variability. As noted in Chapter 3, Pakistan's production variability for its staple food is one of the lowest in the world. Larger fluctuations in domestic availability shorten the expected length of time that the government will have to hold a given quantity of stock, thereby lowering expected holding costs and leading to higher levels of interannual storage.

2. Higher transaction costs for foreign trade. Although the costs of engaging in foreign trade are quite high for Pakistan, costs for many less developed countries, particularly those in Africa, are higher. Higher transaction costs lower the cost of storage relative to the cost of international trade, leading to higher interannual storage.

3. A preference for the domestic staple. In Pakistan there is no consumer preference for domestically produced wheat over imported wheat. White maize consumers, on the other hand, typically have a strong preference for white maize over the yellow maize that dominates international trade. Strong preferences of this type add a third element to the government objective function, a desire to limit imports even when there are no fiscal losses from importing and selling domestically. This provides further incentive for storing excess domestic production across years.

4. A lower own-price elasticity of demand. This parameter for Pakistan was assumed to be quite low at -0.3. Nevertheless, a lower elasticity would decrease the extent to which consumption adjusts when prices change, thus forcing trade and stock changes to absorb more of the production variability.

When several of these parameters change in the same direction, the size of efficient interannual storage could be large. Thus, it would be inappropriate to claim that most countries should avoid holding interannual supply stabilization stocks altogether. The techniques for efficiently stabilizing prices, however, should carry over to other countries. For example, the sensitivity of the domestic price to domestic production and the world price that results from instituting a production or world price bonus payment system usually will result in some gain in efficiency. It is always more costly to stabilize prices completely than to allow some variability. In general, the cost of stabilizing prices increases as complete stability is reached. Since the marginal benefits of stability are in essence politically determined, economists alone are unable to equate marginal benefits with marginal costs. But the measurement of trade-offs between objectives as performed in Chapter 4 is useful for helping to determine the appropriate degree of price variability. As long as the political cost of a 1 percent change in official prices is not infinite, there is some scope for price adjustments.

Although several suggestions have been made here for improving interannual price and storage policy, most governments that are involved in storage operations will discover that the largest single element of storage demand and the largest potential cost-savings are in seasonal rather than interannual policy. This flows mainly from the much greater potential for public displacement of private storage in the seasonal case.

Even in this area, however, the benefits of increasing the gap between government buying and selling prices may be considerably less in other countries. One of the driving forces behind the results for Pakistan is the large loss associated with each ton of wheat handled under present policy. A decrease in the gap increases losses per unit handled *and* increases the volume handled, leading to a large increase in losses. For countries in which the difference between buying and selling prices approximates government costs, the benefits of increasing the gap will be small.

In conclusion, this study has highlighted the three different components of the demand for government storage, which are often confused. In conducting a separate analysis of each of the components, frequently the neglected seasonal component will be the most important. For many countries, the efficient size of interannual supply stabilization stocks may be quite small except in periods of unusually low world prices. A monthly analysis of import buffer stocks is useful for estimating the minimum size of export triggers. These three components constitute the demand for public storage.

APPENDIX 1: SUPPLEMENTARY TABLES

Table 27—Area equation results, by agroclimatic zone

Coefficient	Rice/Wheat Punjab	Mixed Punjab	Cotton/Wheat Punjab	Low-Intensity Punjab	Barani Punjab	Rice/Other Sind	Cotton/Wheat Sind	Other NWFP[a]	Other Baluchistan
Constant	590	252	171	249	233	25.7	79.5	186	20.1
Lagged area, wheat	0.343 (2.25)	0.821 (7.87)	0.699 (5.7)	0.498 (2.04)	0.329 (1.68)	0.381 (2.5)	-0.0263 (-0.11)	0.471 (2.32)	0.230 (1.03)
Expected revenue, wheat	13.58 (2.94)	1.43 (0.432)	1.64 (0.205)	6.71 (1.67)	...	...	-0.906 (-0.32)	8.47 (1.95)	3.33 (2.35)
Procurement price, wheat	...	...	...	...	6.80 (2.78)	-0.432 (-0.08)	...	...	...
Cotton price	...	...	0.184 (0.33)	...	...	...	...	...	...
Expected revenue, cotton	...	...	...	...	...	...	0.904 (0.62)	...	...
IRRI rice price	...	...	...	...	...	3.63 (1.09)	...	...	...
Basmati rice	-3.54 (-1.41)	...	...	...	...	...	...	...	...
Urea price	...	-0.175 (-2.07)	-0.145 (-0.86)	-0.146 (-0.97)	...	-0.0598 (-0.83)	-0.149 (-1.35)	...	0.0609 (0.85)
Rainfall, October	...	...	...	...	0.323 (1.51)	2.38 (2.76)	...	...	...
Rainfall, November	...	1.06 (2.15)	...	...	0.578 (2.53)	...	...	...	...
Rainfall, October/November	...	...	...	...	...	...	...	0.519 (1.21)	...
Rainfall, November/December	...	...	...	...	...	...	...	...	1.19 (3.09)
Expected water availability	...	...	2.12 (2.13)	2.62 (1.14)	...	...	8.37 (4.06)	...	...
Surface water availability, rabi season	...	...	...	...	...	21.27 (2.63)	...	...	...

Table 27—Continued

	...	...	...	...	...	...	...	...
Tubewells							0.00236 (0.3)	
R²	0.82	0.85	0.94	0.85	0.59	0.79	0.95	0.88	0.52
Adjusted R²	0.78	0.81	0.92	0.81	0.46	0.68	0.92	0.85	0.37
Standard error	33.40	26.00	50.00	32.00	12.70	21.30	25.50	26.50	21.80
h-statistic	−0.80	−0.95	−0.32	b	1.10	0.25	b	1.13	0.25

Notes: t-statistics are in parentheses.

Rainfall series for each zone were computed by averaging rainfall stations within each district and then computing a weighted average of the district rainfall by month for each zone, with the weights equal to the share of each district in zonal production.

The series for surface water availability has been created by the author by apportioning the water flowing through individual canals to zones based on the proportion of the canal in each zone. Total water availability adds to the surface water an amount from tubewells, computed by multiplying the number of tubewells in each zone by a standard withdrawal. Expected water availability was constructed from the water availability series by computing a series of five-year trends and projecting those trends one year forward.

The tubewell series for the Other NWFP zone is a constant proportion of the provincial series.

a North-West Frontier Province.
b h-statistic cannot be computed. Durbin-Watson statistic is 2.09.

93

Table 28—Yield equation results, by agroclimatic zone

Coefficient	Rice/Wheat Punjab	Mixed Punjab	Cotton/Wheat Punjab	Low-Intensity Punjab	Barani Punjab	Rice/Other Sind	Cotton/Wheat Sind	Other NWFP[a]	Other Baluchistan
Constant	−0.0242	0.597	0.878	0.230	0.151	−0.285	1.09	0.176	0.0397
Procurement price	0.0420 (1.52)	0.0461 (2.26)	0.0305 (2.05)	0.0420 (1.71)	0.00625 (3.63)	0.0324 (1.25)	−0.00717 (−0.4)	0.0192 (1.14)	0.00400 (0.17)
Fertilizer sales	0.00293 (1.83)	0.00311 (7.04)	0.000877 (3.54)	0.00271 (1.40)	0.02 (3.18)	...	...	0.00449 (2.56)	...
High temperature	−0.0113 (−0.44)	...	−0.0138 (−1.59)	...	...	−0.0103 (−0.58)	...	...	...
Water availability, rabi season	0.00560 (0.88)	...	0.00339 (3.04)	0.00511 (0.95)	...	...	...	...	...
Rainfall, December	...	...	−0.00166 (−1.74)	−0.00358 (−1.95)	...	...	...	...	...
Cotton price	...	...	−0.00196 (−2.04)	...	...	...	−0.00118 (−1.47)	...	...
Temperature	...	...	...	−0.0464 (−1.61)	−0.0316 (−1.9)	...	...	...	...
Rainfall, November	...	...	...	...	0.00310 (3.30)	...	...	...	...
Rainfall, December-February	...	...	...	...	0.000733 (3.69)	...	...	...	...
Square root of tubewells	...	...	...	...	...	0.00643 (6.63)	0.0100 (16.4)	...	...
Surface water availability, rabi season	...	...	...	...	...	0.076 (1.87)	...	...	...
Urea price	...	...	...	...	...	...	−0.000102 (−0.46)	...	...
Tubewells	...	...	...	...	...	...	...	0.00007 (4.1)	0.000131 (3.4)
Rainfall, annual	...	...	...	...	...	...	...	0.000134 (0.58)	0.000982 (1.09)

Table 28—Continued

R²	0.82	0.78	0.89	0.68	0.98	0.90	0.98	0.92	0.88
Adjusted R²	0.77	0.75	0.84	0.54	0.97	0.86	0.97	0.90	0.84
Standard error	0.1200	0.0826	0.0595	0.1000	0.0438	0.1030	0.0640	0.0663	0.1180
Durbin-Watson	1.99	2.52	2.96	1.58	2.01	1.48	1.98	1.62	0.83

Notes: t-statistics are in parentheses.

"High temperature" was computed as an average of the five highest daily highs during a critical 15-day period. The critical period was February 5-20 for Hyderabad and was progressively later for more northern zones. If the average on the five highest days was less than a given critical value, the value of the variable was zero. Otherwise, the value was the average of those five days minus the critical value. The "Temperature" variable is constructed similarly, but uses the average high for March.

The series for surface water availability have been created by the author by apportioning the water flowing through individual canals to zones based on the proportion of the canal in each zone. Total water availability adds to the surface water an amount from tubewells, computed by multiplying the number of tubewells in each zone by a standard withdrawal.

Rainfall series for each zone were computed by averaging rainfall stations within each district and then computing a weighted average of the district rainfall by month for each zone, with the weights equal to the share of each district in zonal production.

The tubewell series for Punjab zones aggregate district data. For Sind, NWFP, and Baluchistan, no district data are available, so the zonal series are constant proportions of provincial data.

[a] North-West Frontier Province.

Table 29—Key parameter values of the interannual models

Parameter	External	Internal
Transactions costs of importing	US$30	Rs170[a]
Transactions costs of exporting	US$-13[b]	Rs646
Shadow price premium on foreign exchange	. . .	10 percent
Discount rate	7 percent	7 percent
Mean production	. . .	13 million metric tons
Coefficient of variation of production	. . .	6 percent
Normal-production-year equilibrium price (rupees per 40 kilograms)	. . .	Rs85
Annual cost of storage per metric ton	. . .	Rs425
Opening world price	US$110	. . .
Standard deviation of world price	US$20	. . .
Own-price demand elasticity	. . .	−0.3

Note: Food aid equals 50 percent of the shortfall in total supply below 12.5 million metric tons, where total supply equals production plus opening government stocks.

[a] For the sake of simplicity, government handling costs of domestic wheat are not explicitly modeled. This allows for the separation conceptually of the costs of subsidies on wheat consumption from the costs of interannual supply stabilization. In the model, this is accomplished by not including a charge for government handling of wheat, and by having the selling price equal the buying price. This necessitates the excess charge for domestic handling of imported wheat over and above the charges on domestically produced wheat.

[b] Lower international transactions for Pakistani wheat as opposed to those for U.S. wheat.

APPENDIX 2: CHOOSING BETWEEN LINEAR AND EXPONENTIAL TRENDS

The following selection procedure was used for selecting between linear and exponential trends:

1. Estimate:
$$Y = a_1 + b_1 T + e_1,$$

where Y is the dependent vector, T is the time vector, and e_1 is the vector of residuals of the linear trend.

2. Estimate:
$$\log Y = a_2 + b_2 T + u_1,$$

where u_1 is the vector of residuals of the exponential trend.

3. Compute the residuals of the transformed fitted values for both equations:

$$e_2 = \log Y - \log(a_1 + b_1 T),$$
$$u_2 = Y - \exp(a_2 + b_2 T),$$

where exp( ) is the exponential function (taking antilogs).

The linear equation is the better fit if the sum of squared residuals of the linear equation is less than the sum of squared residuals of the log-linear equation in both linear and logarithmic space:

$$e_2' e_2 < u_1' u_1 \quad \text{and} \quad e_1' e_1 < u_2' u_2.$$

The exponential equation is the better fit if

$$u_2' u_2 < e_1' e_1 \quad \text{and} \quad u_1' u_1 < e_2' e_2.$$

Otherwise, the problem is indeterminate. In this case, we chose the exponential trend if

$$u_2' u_2 / e_1' e_1 < e_2' e_2 / u_1' u_1.$$

APPENDIX 3: EQUATIONS FOR INTERANNUAL OPTIMIZATION PROBLEM

The structure of the optimization problem in Chapter 4 is as follows:

State variables:

WP = world price,

Q = production, and

GS = opening government stocks.

Control variables:

NP = procurement minus offtake,
or net procurement,

M = imports, and

X = exports.

State transition equations:

(1) Q is an exogenous random variable, uncorrelated with past values for Q.

(2) WP moves in a random walk in the simulations. In the discrete world of dynamic programming, a random walk is not feasible without an unacceptably large number of allowable values for WP. The probabilities of moving from one level of WP to another are chosen so that the expected value of next year's price is never more than US$7 per ton above or below the present year's price.

(3) $GS_{t+1} = GS_t + NP_t + M_t - X_t$.

Behavioral equation:

The government chooses NP, which then determines price through the following two equations for consumption C:

$$C = Q - NP, \text{ and}$$
$$C = A \cdot P^e,$$

where A is a constant, P is the market price, and e is the own-price demand elasticity.

Objective function:

Minimize present and discounted future values of the following function:

$$GC = FC + aPV,$$

where GC is government cost (including financial costs and perceived costs of price variability), FC is fiscal cost, "a" is a weighting parameter, and PV is a measure of price variability.

Government fiscal cost, FC, is the sum of within-country operations, WCC, foreign trade costs, FTC, storage costs, SC, and a charge for the net change in value of stocks on hand over each 10-year cycle, RST:

$$FC = WCC + FTC + SC + RST,$$

$$WCC = P \cdot NP, \quad and$$

$$FTC = M(WP + MC) - AID \cdot WP - X(WP - XC),$$

where MC is the costs of importing, AID is food aid, and XC is the costs of exporting. Foreign exchange components of WP, MC, and XC are valued at a 10 percent premium above domestic components. Food aid, AID, is a set percentage of the shortfall in total supply below a certain level:

$$AID_t = 0.5[(Q^* - 500) - (Q_t + GS_t)],$$

where Q^* is normal production, and values are expressed in thousand tons. This formulation for food aid yields values somewhat lower than has occurred in the past. In some runs of the model presented in Chapter 4, AID is assumed to be zero.

The third element of fiscal cost is storage costs, modeled as an average cost STCOST per ton stored:

$$SC = STCOST \cdot GS.$$

The final element in fiscal cost values the change in stock from the beginning to the end of the cycle. If this is not included, policies that lower stock levels over time will appear more profitable than they should. The valuation of the stock change, however, should not depend on the random variable WP in the terminal year; that would be equivalent to forcing the exportation of all stocks, thus penalizing the optimal policies that hold more stocks in years of low world prices. Thus the stocks are always valued at the base year world price, regardless of the terminal year price:

$$RST = (GS_0 - GS_{10})WP_0.$$

Price variability, PV, is measured as the squared deviation from the target price, P^*:

$$PV = (P_t - P^*)^2.$$

The parameter "a" is varied in different optimization runs to map out the trade-off curve between price variability and fiscal cost.

For a more complete description of a similar model and a defense of this type of specification, see Pinckney (1988b, 31-49). The Fortran programs used in the optimization run on IBM PCs are available from the author on request.

APPENDIX 4: MARKETING COSTS

The total cost shown in Table 30, Rs740 million, averaged over the nationwide offtake of 3.7 million tons, is Rs200 per ton, the figure given in Table 31. Figures for North-West Frontier Province (NWFP) are detailed in Tables 32 and 33.

Table 30—Marketing costs to farflung areas, 1986/87

Area	Cost per Metric Ton	Quantity	Total Cost
	(Rs)	(million metric tons)	(Rs million)
Azad Kashmir, Northern Areas, Defense	400	0.4	160
Baluchistan	600	0.3	180
North-West Frontier Province (NWFP)	360	0.8	288
Karachi	225	0.5	112
Total	...	2.0	740

Sources: The costs are computed primarily from Agroprogress Kienbaum International BmbH and Indus Associated Consultants Ltd., "Foodgrains Storage and Processing Study," Annex 3.5.1 (report prepared for the Ministry of Food, Agriculture, and Cooperatives, Islamabad, 1986, Mimeographed); also Punjab Food Department and Pakistan Agricultural Supply and Storage Corporation (PASSCO) expenses for 1985/86 and 1986/87.

Table 31—Marketing costs of buying and selling, 1986/87

Type of Cost	Cost per Metric Ton
	(Rs)
Costs of Buying	
Fumigation	2
Bags	160
Delivery charges	10
Transport to storage center	8
Handling at storage center	10
Variable costs component of godown expenses and departmental charges	30
Total	220
Costs of Selling	
Handling during removal from storage	10
Costs of marketing and transport within Punjab and Sind	70
Average costs of transport and handling to farflung areas	200
Total	280

Sources: The costs are computed primarily from Agroprogress Kienbaum International BmbH and Indus Associated Consultants Ltd., "Foodgrains Storage and Processing Study," Annex 3.5.1 (report prepared for the Ministry of Food, Agriculture, and Cooperatives, Islamabad, 1986, Mimeographed); also Punjab Food Department and Pakistan Agricultural Supply and Storage Corporation (PASSCO) expenses for 1985/86 and 1986/87.

Table 32—Rates for transportation of wheat from Punjab to North-West Frontier Province, 1986/87

From Punjab to	Lowest Rate Approved per Metric Ton per Kilometer (Net Weight)
	(paisa)
Peshawar District	28.75
Mardan District	29.11
Kohat District	29.75
Abbottabad District	28.74
Mansehra District	31.95
Dargai Malakand Agency	29.74
Swat District	31.94
Bannu District	38.00
D. I. Khan District	40.99
Karak District	30.45

Source: North-West Frontier Province (NWFP) Food Department.

Table 33—Costs of transportation and incidentals for wheat handling in North-West Frontier Province, 1984/85-1986/87

	1984/85		1985/86		1986/87	
	By Rail	By Road	By Rail	By Road	By Rail	By Road
	(Rs/metric ton)					
Transportation	50.01	262.90	48.73	286.28	51.17	300.59
Handling charges	1.28	1.28	1.63	1.63	1.71	1.71
Tax and duties	3.63	3.63	3.63	3.63	3.63	3.63
Godown expenses	6.72	6.72	1.45	1.45	1.52	1.52
Miscellaneous charges	12.79	12.79	14.16	14.16	14.87	14.87
Repair to storage bins	2.78	2.78	2.62	2.62	2.75	2.75
Storage surcharge	2.68	2.68	2.62	2.62	2.75	2.75
Interest	84.64	84.64	29.37	29.37	29.37	29.37
Railway freight	184.42	. . .	254.51	. . .	254.51	. . .
Total	348.95	377.42	358.72	341.76	362.28	357.19

Source: North-West Frontier Province (NWFP) Food Department.

In addition to these costs, the government incurs fixed costs per unit of storage capacity. These total about Rs80 per ton per year according to the Agroprogress and Indus (1986) study, and include permanent staff, electricity, depreciation, and other costs that do not go down if the facility is not used. These costs are not included in the model. To the extent that a change in policy allows for a smaller government storage capacity, further savings would be incurred through a decrease in these fixed costs.

APPENDIX 5: SUPPLEMENTARY FIGURES

Figure 13—Actual and estimated prices of wheat in Pakistan, 1985/86

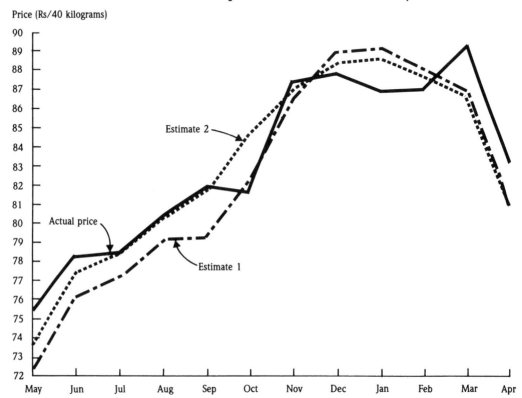

Note: Estimate 1 uses the original values of the A parameter listed in Table 20, after adjusting for population growth. Estimate 2 uses the revised values of the A parameter from the same table, again adjusting for population growth.

Figure 14—Actual and estimated prices of wheat in Pakistan, 1986/87

Price (Rs/40 kilograms)

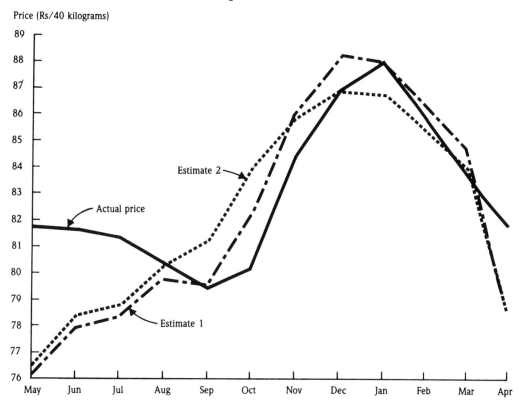

Note: Estimate 1 uses the original values of the A parameter listed in Table 20, after adjusting for population growth. Estimate 2 uses the revised values of the A parameter from the same table, again adjusting for population growth.

Figure 15—Actual and estimated private storage of wheat in Pakistan, 1985/86

Private Storage (million metric tons)

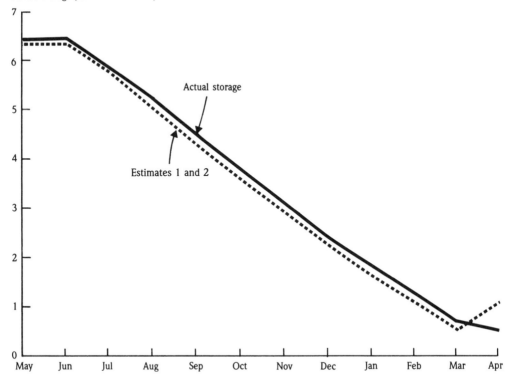

Note: Estimate 1 uses the original values of the A parameter listed in Table 20, after adjusting for population growth. Estimate 2 uses the revised values of the A parameter from the same table, again adjusting for population growth.

Figure 16—Actual and estimated private storage of wheat in Pakistan, 1986/87

Private Storage (million metric tons)

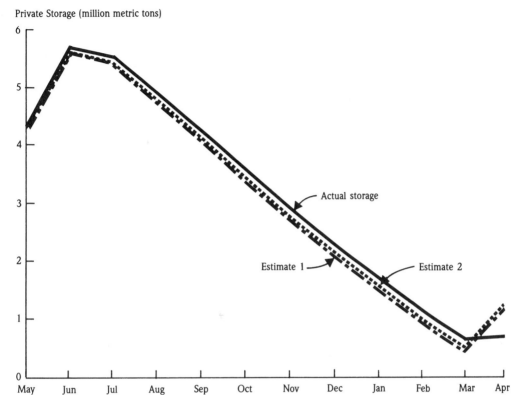

Note: Estimate 1 uses the original values of the A parameter listed in Table 20, after adjusting for population growth. Estimate 2 uses the revised values of the A parameter from the same table, again adjusting for population growth.

APPENDIX 6: FINANCING IMPORTS

Under any policy, there will be times when the opening supply stabilization stocks of the country are insufficient to meet the shortfall in supply because of random yield fluctuations. Such situations will require the use of foreign exchange for imports and the use of food aid. Although holding no interannual supply stabilization stocks may maximize net foreign exchange earnings in the long run, it can exacerbate the short-run problem of arranging for imports in deficit years.

The international community has attempted to address this difficulty and the parallel problem of a major production shortfall in an export crop. The Compensatory Financing Facility (CFF) of the International Monetary Fund (IMF) was introduced in 1963 to mitigate the adverse effect of export instability on the balance of payments of the countries that export primary commodities. The principal purpose has been to provide timely relief to members with payment difficulties arising from temporary shortfalls in their export earnings due to factors largely out of their control. The assumption is that these payment difficulties are only temporary and do not require policy reforms. The amount of the drawing is constrained by the size of the calculated shortfall, subject to a limit on outstanding drawings. The interest rate charged on CFF drawings is the same as that applied to other drawings from the IMF.

While the underlying rationale for the use of the CFF has not changed since 1963, there have been major changes in the scope and method of its operation. These changes include the commodity coverage of the facility, method of calculation, and maximum level of drawing. The CFF is not commodity specific, and shortfalls are related to total export earnings, including services such as workers' remittances. The drawings under the CFF are additional to what a member might draw under the normal lending facilities of the IMF. However, the maximum permissible amount of drawings has varied in terms of the members' quota limit. Periodic quota increases have allowed a substantial increase in maximum drawings in absolute terms.

In 1981, the CFF coverage was extended by permitting the optional inclusion of a temporary increase in the cost of commercial cereal imports. The objective of the Cereal Imports Excesses (CIE) provision is to minimize the effects of foreign exchange availability constraints by making loans to member countries that experience temporary surges in cereal import bills, thereby avoiding downward fluctuations in food consumption or inappropriate and costly policy adjustments.

Under the CIE the amount of a drawing is calculated as the sum of the export shortfall and cereal imports increase, with the total subject to limits on outstanding drawings. The shortfall is calculated in relation to a trend, defined as an average of the value of exports and cereal imports for five years, centered on the year of the export shortfall (or excess cereal imports). The trend calculation thus requires forecasts for cereal imports and total exports for two years into the future.

The CIE has a number of advantages over alternative food security schemes. It is less political than food aid, does not require any international agreement, allows countries to rely on imports rather than stockholding, and (at least in principle) can be immediately responsive to cereal production fluctuations or changes in the world price (Huddleston et al. 1984).

For some countries, the actual experience of the CIE has not met expectations, as the assistance provided has been deemed inadequate in relation to need. Supporters of this view suggest that the CIE should be the primary means by which food consumption shortfalls are met and that any corollary features of the provision that interfere with such an objective are counterproductive. Others argue that the CIE has not yet been tested because of low world prices since 1981, minimal shortfalls in cereal production, and abundance of food aid (which is cheaper than using the CIE).

One technical problem with the CIE arises from an IMF decision in 1983 integrating the CFF to the highly conditional financing of the upper credit tranches. Drawings on lower tranches now require a mission to assess whether policy adjustments may be necessary to address balance-of-payments difficulties. Drawings in upper tranches require the existence of a "satisfactory" balance-of-payments position or the existence of a broadly "satisfactory" performance under arrangement with the IMF.

Determination of the origin of a shortfall is straightforward when it is due to changes in international prices. The assessment is more difficult when changes stem from variations in quantities exported or imported or both. This is where cooperation requirements for drawings between the member country and the IMF become more influential. Since 1966, drawings that represent a relatively large percentage of a member's Fund quota (upper tranche) have become subject to increasingly higher levels of conditionality than drawings from a lower tranche. Particularly in the 1980s, long-term balance-of-payments difficulties have emerged that overshadow temporary shortfalls in export earnings or increases in cereal imports. This change in emphasis has affected the guidelines for drawing from the CFF and the CIE provision in both the lower and upper tranches.

Under current conditions, it is difficult to separate the effects of general balance-of-payments difficulties from those of export shortfalls or cereal import excesses. Concurrently, lower world prices for cereals and higher levels of food aid have guaranteed lower levels of drawings under the CIE provision.

A further element of uncertainty with regard to a country's eligibility under the CIE provision is introduced by the lack of clear definitions as to what is a "satisfactory" balance-of-payments position. Thus, the semiautomatic basis on which the CIE drawings were supposed to be made has to some extent been abolished during the recent years of acute overall balance-of-payments difficulties for so many less-developed countries (LDCs).

Currently, the interest charge on CIE drawings is 6 percent—low in comparison with international capital markets but high in comparison with the economic cost of food aid to recipient countries. The debt burden of so many LDCs today is a strong deterrent against expanding their foreign debt through such drawings. Nevertheless, the cost of the CIE is considerably less than the cost of building larger buffer stocks.

The CIE provision was reviewed in both 1985 and 1987, but no major changes in policy have been agreed upon. Possible modifications of the provision proposed for discussion at the 1987 review included liberalizing the conditions for low-income LDCs by reducing the interest charges and relaxing the three-year repayment rule. It was also hoped that discussions might focus on a complete divorce of the CIE provision from the CFF. This initiative had been proposed in 1981 but was rejected on the grounds that increased export revenues could offset excess import costs, thereby nullifying any potential balance-of-payments problems. These same issues will no doubt be those raised in any future review (one is scheduled for mid-1989), but the same factions are as strongly entrenched in their positions now as ever, and thus the prospect of major revisions seems unlikely at this point.

In sum, the CIE provision is one possibility for assisting Pakistan in years of shortfalls in wheat production. Although it is not ideal, the facility does provide foreign exchange for imports during periods when availability may be a problem.

BIBLIOGRAPHY

Agroprogress Kienbaum International BmbH and Indus Associated Consultants Ltd. 1986. Foodgrain storage and processing study. A report prepared for the Ministry of Food, Agriculture, and Cooperatives, Islamabad. Mimeo.

Ahmed, E., H.M. Leung, and N. Stern. 1986. Demand for wheat under nonlinear pricing in Pakistan. London School of Economics, London. Mimeo.

Alderman, Harold. 1988a. Estimates of consumer price response in Pakistan using market prices as data. *Pakistan Development Review* 27 (Summer): 89-107.

_____. 1988b.The twilight of wheat flour rationing in Pakistan. *Food Policy* 13 (August): 245-256.

Alderman, Harold, M. Ghaffar Chaudhry, and Marito Garcia. 1988. *Household food security in Pakistan: The ration shop system.* Working Papers on Food Subsidies 4. Washington, D.C.: International Food Policy Research Institute and Pakistan Institute of Development Economics.

Arzac, Enrique R., and Maurice Wilkinson. 1980. Dynamic analysis and optimal control of agricultural commodity markets. In *Applied stochastic control in econometrics and management science,* ed. Alain Bensoussan, Paul Kleindorfer, and Charles Tapiero, 41-77. Amsterdam: North Holland.

Brennan, Michael J. 1958. The supply of storage. *American Economic Review* 48: 50-72.

Cheema, A. A., and M. H. Malik. 1985. Changes in consumption patterns and employment under alternative income distribution in Pakistan. *Pakistan Development Review* 24 (Spring): 1-22.

Cornelisse, Peter A., and Syed Nawab Haider Naqvi. 1984. *The anatomy of the wheat market in Pakistan.* Rotterdam: Erasmus University, and Islamabad: Pakistan Institute of Development Economics.

Dorosh, Paul, and Alberto Valdés. 1989. Effects of exchange rate and trade policies on agricultural incentives and output in Pakistan. International Food Policy Research Institute, Washington, D.C. Mimeo.

Experience Incorporated, Zor Engineers (Private) Ltd., and Ferguson and Associates. 1986. Godown rehabilitation, recurrent cost analysis and management audit of public sector grain storage, phase I. A report prepared for the U.S. Agency for International Development, Washington, D.C. Mimeo.

Gardner, Bruce. 1979. *Optimal stockpiling of grain.* Lexington, Mass., U.S.A.: Lexington Books.

Gray, Roger W., and Anne E. Peck. 1981. The Chicago wheat futures markets: Recent problems in historical perspective. *Food Research Institute Studies* 18 (1): 89-115.

Gustafson, Robert L. 1958. Carryover levels for grains: A method for determining amounts that are optimal under specified conditions. *Technical Bulletin* 1178: 48-49. U.S. Department of Agriculture, Washington, D.C.

Hamid, Naved, Thomas C. Pinckney, Suzanne Gnaegy, and Alberto Valdés. 1987. The wheat economy of Pakistan: Setting and prospects. A report submitted to the U.S. Agency for International Development. International Food Policy Research Institute, Washington, D.C. Mimeo.

Hazell, Peter B.R. 1982. *Instability in Indian foodgrain production.* Research Report 30. Washington, D.C.: International Food Policy Research Institute.

_____. 1984. Sources of increased instability in Indian and U.S. cereal production. *American Journal of Agricultural Economics* 66 (August): 302-311.

_____. 1988. Changing pattern of variability in cereal prices and production. In *Agricultural price policy for developing countries,* ed. John W. Mellor and Raisuddin Ahmed, 27-52. Baltimore, Md., U.S.A.: Johns Hopkins University Press for the International Food Policy Research Institute.

Huddleston, Barbara, D. Gale Johnson, Shlomo Reutlinger, and Alberto Valdés. 1984. *International finance for food security.* Baltimore, Md., U.S.A.: Johns Hopkins University Press for the World Bank.

Josling, Timothy. 1981. Price, stock, and trade policies and the functioning of international grain markets. In *Food security for developing countries,* ed. Alberto Valdés, 161-184. Boulder, Colo., U.S.A.: Westview Press.

Lowry, Mark, Joseph Glauber, Mario Miranda, and Peter Helmberger. 1987. Pricing and storage of field crops: A quarterly model applied to soybeans. *American Journal of Agricultural Economics* 69 (November): 740-749.

Massell, Benton F. 1969. Price stabilization and welfare. *Quarterly Journal of Economics* 83 (2): 284-298.

Mellor, John W. 1978. Food price policy and income distribution in low-income countries. *Economic Development and Cultural Change* 27 (October): 1-26.

Michel, Aloys A. 1967. *The Indus rivers: A study of the effects of partition.* New Haven, Conn., U.S.A.: Yale University Press.

Oi, Walter Y. 1961. The desirability of price instability under perfect competition. *Econometrica* 29 (January): 58-64.

Pakistan. 1971/72, 1979, 1984/85. *Household income and expenditure survey.* Karachi: Federal Bureau of Statistics.

_____. 1985. *Agricultural statistics of Pakistan.* Islamabad: Ministry of Food, Agriculture, and Cooperatives, Food and Agriculture Division.

_____. Various years. *Wheat situation report.* Islamabad: Ministry of Food, Agriculture, and Cooperatives, Planning Unit, Early Warning System Project.

Pakistan Agricultural Research Council. 1986. Increasing wheat productivity in the context of Pakistan's irrigated cropping systems: A view from the farmer's field. PARC/CIMMYT Collaborative Project Paper 86/7. PARC, Islamabad. Mimeo.

Peck, Anne E. 1977-78. Implications of private storage of grains for buffer stock schemes to stabilize prices. *Food Research Institute Studies* 16 (3): 125-140.

Pinckney, Thomas C. 1988a. The effects of pricing policy on seasonal storage of wheat in Pakistan. International Food Policy Research Institute, Washington, D.C. Mimeo.

_____. 1988b. *Storage, trade, and price policy under production instability: Maize in Kenya.* Research Report 71. Washington, D.C.: International Food Policy Research Institute.

_____. 1988c. Wheat storage policy in Pakistan: Implications of price policy and production instability. International Food Policy Research Institute, Washington, D.C. Mimeo.

_____. 1989. The multiple effects of procurement price on production and procurement of wheat in Pakistan. *Pakistan Development Review* 28 (2): 95-119.

Samuelson, Paul A. 1972. The consumer does benefit from feasible price stability. *Quarterly Journal of Economics* 86 (August): 476-493.

Siamwalla, Ammar. 1988. Public stock management. In *Agricultural Price Policy for Developing Countries,* ed. John W. Mellor and Raisuddin Ahmed, 81-93. Baltimore, Md., U.S.A.: Johns Hopkins University Press for the International Food Policy Research Institute.

Waugh, Frederick V. 1944. Does the consumer benefit from price instability? *Quarterly Journal of Economics* 58 (August): 602-614.

Working, Holbrook. 1949. The theory of price of storage. *The American Economic Review* 39: 1254-1262.

Wright, Brian D., and Jeffrey C. Williams. 1988. Measurement of consumer gains from market stabilization. *American Journal of Agricultural Economics* 70 (August): 616-627.